WHEN
YOU DON'T
AGREE

WHEN YOU DON'T AGREE

James G. T. Fairfield

HERALD PRESS
Scottdale, Pennsylvania
Kitchener, Ontario

When You Don't Agree was outlined and developed by a task force appointed jointly by Mennonite Broadcasts, Inc. Harrisonburg, Virginia, and the Congregational Literature and Herald Press divisions of Mennonite Publishing House, Scottdale, Pennsylvania

Quotations marked NEB are from *The New English Bible.* © The Delegates of the Oxford University Press and The Syndics of the Cambridge University Press 1961, 1970. Reprinted by Permission.

Quotations marked "Phillips" are from *The New Testament in Modern English*, Revised Edition. © J. B. Phillips 1958, 1960, 1972. By permission of Macmillan Publishing Co., Inc. and William Collins Sons & Co., Ltd.

Quotations marked RSV are from the Revised Standard Version of the Bible, copyrighted 1946, 1952, © 1971, 1973.

Quotations marked TEV are from *Good News for modern Man* (TEV). Copyright © by American Bible Society, 1966, 1971. Used by permission.

Quotations marked NIV are from *The New International Version, New Testament.* Copyright © 1973 by New York Bible Society International. Used by permission.

Contents

Preface: How Do You Handle Conflict? 7

Part I. Common Conflict Styles
   1. The Presence of Conflict 15
   2. Defining Conflict 18
   3. Five Conflict Styles 21
   4. The Long View of Conflict 30
   5. Which Style Is More Valuable? 30
   6. Analyze Your Progress 41
   7. In Hope of Change 47

Part II. Improving Communication Skills
   8. Some Problems in Speaking 55
   9. Meanings Are Inside 60
  10. Sending and Perceiving a Message 64
  11. Improving Your Sending Skills 70
  12. The Art of Listening 80
  13. Analyze Your Progress 89

Part III. A Larger Love
  14. The Different Kinds of Love 99
  15. The Strength of Self-Giving Love 107
  16. Skills of Self-Giving Love
       (A) Forgiveness: Respects and Trusts 113

17. Skills of Self-Giving Love
    (B) Compassion: Discerns and Cares 123
18. Skills of Self-Giving Love
    (C) Responsibility: Decides and Acts 128
19. Self-Giving Love in Marriage 135

Part IV. Confronting Your Problem
    20. Knowing Your Feelings 147
    21. The Problem of Anger 163
    22. "I" and "You" Messages 168
    23. Helping the Other Person 181

Part V. Setting New Conflict Patterns
    24. Daring to Change 193
    25. Seven Characteristics of Creative Conflict 199
    26. Some Additional Destructive Tactics 206
    27. Plan for a Constructive Conflict 213
    28. Improve on Your Conflicts.................222

Part VI. Putting It Together
    29. Where You Have Been....................229
    30. Six Equal Rights 234
    31. Skills and Integrity, A Personal View 240

Selected Bibliography 245
The Author 247

Preface:

How Do You Handle Conflict?

Do you know how to handle conflict? When unwelcome pressure comes from your boss or your neighbor or your spouse, do you know how to cope with it in a positive way?

Or like a lot of us, do you burn up inside with internalized frustration? The way we respond to conflict can determine our lifestyle, our freedom, and even our sanity.

This book is a brief manual on how to handle conflicts with the least amount of strain on relationships while achieving personal growth.

A number of helpful books are available on one or more aspects of why we quarrel, and how we should go about it. But the publishing group behind *When You Don't Agree* felt a need to pull together a number of the basic concepts and skills in resolving conflicts so that in one study the reader could get a handle on his or her own conflict situations.

As you will note from the table of contents, we will first explore the ways people customarily approach conflict so that you can see your own methods in contrast to the styles other people use. In part two we will study the problems—and the possibilities—of clear communication in conflict.

Next we deal with the motives behind conflict, and the working value of a tough-minded love. And this leads us into a section on anger and feelings and how to control their effect on us in conflict situations.

Then with the clearer understanding you will have reached at this point, you can practice some techniques of improving your conflicts in part five. And a final section puts it together as a lifestyle from the writer's point of view.

This is a book to write in, so go ahead and write in it! Read it in easy stages by yourself or study it with a friend or a group. Whichever way you choose, *let the book serve you.*

We designed it to give you some actual practice as you go along, through simulated situations and questions about them. Also questions follow whenever a segment introduces new concepts and skills. As you respond to the questions and think through the answers we explain, we hope you will find yourself enjoying the experience as well as getting more out of the concepts.

One problem: the answer to each exercise appears in italics immediately following each set of questions. That means you may see the answer before you want to. Covering the answer with your hand or a piece of paper will help. If inadvertently you do see the answer, don't feel guilty about it. The idea isn't to put you back in school with tests and grades, but to make the material clearer and more helpful to you. So enjoy yourself!

My principle source in writing this book has been

David W. Augsburger, who was my guide through the basic skills of conflict resolution. Dave took his doctorate in counseling at Claremont, served on the faculty of Northern Baptist Seminary in Chicago, and teaches now at Associated Mennonite Biblical Seminaries, Elkhart, Indiana. For several years until we both moved into other areas, Dave and I worked together at Mennonite Broadcasts, Inc., Harrisonburg, Virginia, the public communications arm of the Mennonite Church. Our association then gave me the opportunity now to work on the project with his guidance. It has been both a privilege and a learning experience.

Dave outlined the strategies of conflict resolution, dug in his files, talked his experiences, listed resources, shared lecture notes, and criticized the manuscript carefully as it took shape.

We believe the book can provide readers with some insights into their own responses to conflict. For some readers it may help chart the way to a new internalized system of relating to others. In conflicts we hope to encourage many to fight a good fight that can lead to satisfactory resolutions. And since differences are part of the cost of a relationship, we want to develop an appreciation for differences as part of the color and harmony in a relationship too.

For some readers this book may seem disastrous—in trying the skills we outline, you may seem only to sink into deeper and hotter water in your conflicts. Even so it will fulfill a purpose *if you have been encouraged to look for something better.* To you we declare there *is* a way of harmony and peace in your relationships and we encourage you to stick with your desire *and seek professional counsel.* Ask your family doctor whom he would recommend for counsel. Talk to the family bureau if you have one, or the mental health representatives in your area or mail one of the response cards included in this book following pages 96 and 248. *Don't give up.* Conflicts can bear good fruit. Your life can shift from frustration and dissatisfaction to a new experience of personal growth and healthier relationships.

As you will see, my chosen point of view is Christian. For me that means trusting that God *is*, however indescribable He may be. Furthermore, I believe He has taken steps to reveal Himself across the eternity-gap, both in historical acts to a chosen audience—the descendants of Abraham—and in Jesus, born to human parents.

It appears to me that His principle reason for communicating with us was to make known the character of reality, the "nature" of nature and humanity, and where we have been and where we are going. The short description of Him in the Bible, "God is love," gives us His motive as well as His method in working to return us to His reality from our less-than-real way of living. And my Christian viewpoint believes that living his way has a great deal to do with how you and I get along with each other in spite of our differences.

As I said, that is my perspective. How you approach the material is your point of view, and whether secularist or a follower of another religion, there is much in the book for you to explore. And if you choose to make this a personal pen-and-paper study, you will benefit from using a Bible as a reference and resource, preferably a modern translation. The Bible is important to a study of conflict, as it is with any attempt to understand our human situation.

When You Don't Agree is the product of the efforts of many people. There are the numbers of volunteers who tested the material in its first and second drafts to see if the content was understandable. These helpful friends asked themselves the questions and risked the answers so we could rephrase the material that missed being clear and communicative.

Others served on a task force called by the publisher's representative, Laurence Martin. These included Kenneth Weaver and David Thompson of Mennonite Broadcasts, Inc. Their interests in correspondence courses sparked the need for this particular study. Keith Yoder, professor of education, Millersville State College, Millersville, Pennsylvania, advised on many aspects of programming the material in questions and answers. Paul M. Zehr represented the Eastern Mennonite Board of Missions. Maynard W. Shetler and Paul M. Schrock spoke for Herald Press. We are also indebted to John Henry Hess, Orval Shoemaker, Jim Gaede, and Donald B. Kraybill who coordinated testing of the material. The typing skills of Sara Ann Showalter and Twila Lehman made the testing of the manuscript possible.

I am most of all indebted to my wife, Norma, and her willing participation in growing together in the intensified conflict experience that is marriage. We have grown "too soon old and too late smart" as the proverb has it. But from the beginning we have had the determination to make love work. To those people who are likewise determined to work through their conflicts to newer and better relationships, this book is dedicated.

James G. T. Fairfield

Part I
Common Conflict Styles

1
The Presence of Conflict

"I'd like Colin to help me with the housework."
Karen's face is blank; she is too emotionally involved in
what she is saying to show her anger.

"I work all day and when I get home I make supper.
Not that I mind that, honestly. I like to cook. He'll help
clear off the table. But then he goes out and works on the
car. And I resent it.

"I've nagged enough about it now that it's an issue
between us. And I'm beginning to see other things I
don't think I like about him. What am I going to do?"

Colin is looking for another job. He doesn't feel he can
survive the tensions and frustrations that go with his
present employment.

"I really like my work. But my boss is insufferable.
The man has no idea of how to handle people—at least
not me!

"I think he believes the worst all the time. And he
won't let me in on what I'm supposed to do next. He
changes my orders right in the middle of a job, with no
explanation. I think he does it deliberately just to upset
me."

Colin's reactions are to bottle up his hostility and look for a new job. Unfortunately he has not been able to find one. Further, although it is obvious the boss is both authoritarian and indecisive, it appears some of Colin's fellow workers do not have the conflicts he is having.

Colin despises himself for knuckling under to his boss and that is adding the last straw to his load. He faces increasing emotional stress unless he deals positively with his situation.

Karen feels she cannot communicate her feelings to her husband. Colin is struggling with his side of an ongoing conflict which may cost him his health.

To us there may seem to be obvious answers for their situations. Colin could stand up to his boss, whether he has found a new job or not—an easier solution for us to offer than for Colin to risk doing. And Karen could tell her husband she resents him playing with the car while she has to do the dishes, right? But maybe Karen isn't as interested as she might be in keeping their car running. So the problem could be a difference in perspective.

As long as there are people in our lives, we will have differences. And conflicts. That fact need not disturb us, because conflicts and differences can be opportunities to improve our lives, providing that we can learn how to manage their influence upon us. How we react to conflict situations can be helpful—or hurtful—depending on our system of handling differences.

And that is what Part I of this book is about, common conflict styles. As you finish this section of the book, you should be able to describe the five most common ways people cope with conflict. You will also be able to pick out the way which matches your usual style of reacting.

Further, you will have the opportunity to identify which other ways you normally fall back on when your first style doesn't suit the situation. Then you can begin to consider the most effective ways of coping with conflict.

Now although we have not moved into the content of Part I as yet, let's try an easy sample of the questions you will meet along the way.

According to what we hope will happen in your reading, by the end of Part I you will be able to describe (how many?) common ways people use to cope with conflict.

In Part I we will explore five ways of responding to conflict.

Depending on our system of handling differences (select one of the following to finish the statement):

_____ a. Conflicts show us up for what we are.
_____ b. Conflicts can be opportunities for growth.
_____ c. Conflicts usually mean we can't handle our emotions.

Too many times our conflicts confuse rather than reveal our personalities, so (a) is not as reliable an answer as (b). As we will see, each conflict can be an opportunity for growth personally as well as in our relationships. Answer (c) is incorrect because it sees conflict as abnormal, which simply is not true.

2
Defining Conflict

conflict (kon´flikt) L. *conflictus*, to strike together. 1: a fight, clash, contention. 2: sharp disagreement or opposition, as of interests, ideas, etc., mutual interference of incompatible forces or wills.

Here are several ways conflict in human relationships has been explained by others.

From his work in conflict resolution, Jay Hall has developed a definition which says that conflict exists whenever there are important differences between people, groups, or communities which, should they persist and remain unresolved, serve to keep the parties involved apart in some way.

According to Harvey Seifert and Howard Clinebell, conflict is a sharper clash of desires than is usually found in a rational exploration of differences between persons or groups. Instead of mutually assisting one another in a problem-solving approach to differences, conflict involves struggle for power and control or for the satisfaction of one's own needs.

Conflict exists as a reality in any relationship and is bound to occur just because people think differently and have differing needs. Thomas Gordon, who developed

Parent Effectiveness Training, describes conflict as a moment of truth in a relationship—a test of its health which can either weaken or strengthen it. Conflicts can push people away from each other or pull them closer together. Between groups, conflicts can either develop into armed warfare or into deeper understanding.

As the chart below suggests, *unresolved* conflicts tend to grow from minor to major, little to big, less to more, cold war to hot:

Difference of opinion	"Spat"	Confrontation
Heated debate or argument	"Quarrel"	Division
Intense physical anger	"Fight"	Rejection
Hostility confirmed	"War"	Separation

"What causes conflicts and quarrels among you? Do they not spring from the aggressiveness of your bodily desires? You want something which you cannot have, and so you are bent on murder; you are envious, and cannot attain your ambition, and so you quarrel and fight. You do not get what you want, because you do not pray for it. Or, if you do, your requests are not granted because you pray from wrong motives" (James 4:1-3, NEB).

Now considering the previous statements, write your own definition of conflict:

Your answer should at least include the concepts of (1) unresolved differences or power struggles which also (2) create problems or distance in human relationships. If your answer does not include both the above, you'll want to look over the definitions again.

To differ from someone else is natural, normal, neutral, and even delightful. Although it can turn into a painful situation with perhaps a sad ending, it doesn't need to.

So conflict of itself is neither good nor bad, right nor wrong. Conflict simply is. *It is how we respond to conflict that creates the problems for us.* And how we approach and work through our differences to a large extent determines the patterns we use to deal with most of the situations in our lives.

3
Five Conflict Styles

If I tend to view conflict as a hopeless inevitability on the human scene which I can do little to control, then I may not even try. "People can't seem to do anything without a quarrel. And it's too hard to try to understand each other. I don't like the strain of hassles, so I avoid a fight. I don't care what other people think; they can do what they like." This style is *Can't win—so I withdraw,* or in short WITHDRAW. It can mean actual physical withdrawal, or an inner psychological turning away from conflict.

Billie and her husband, Paul, began having major problems when Paul took a second job on weekends. Billie worked during the week and felt they had enough income. But Paul's chief reason for taking a weekend job wasn't money. Two days of laundry and housecleaning and shopping with his wife created tensions he couldn't cope with. His weekend job takes him out of these conflicts—even though his WITHDRAW strategy has created another major problem for their marriage.

If the idea of losing conflicts threatens my self-image and world-view I will likely fight to win at all costs. "It's the only way to survive, to look after your own interests. Nobody else is likely to, and if I'm not strong, I'll let you and everybody else down, including God and truth. I must be right or we're all wrong." This style is *Must win—or all is lost,* or WIN. Relationships are secondary. The important thing is to WIN your point of view.

Gordon has been fired again. In his late thirties, he tells the clerk at the employment office, "There aren't too many new tricks for this old dog to learn." So he will try for a dishwasher's job again most likely. He was fired for verbally abusing the night-cook at the restaurant where he worked. The night-cook tried to negotiate a dispute between Gordon and a busboy who wasn't working the way Gordon wanted him to.

"I don't believe in letting those kids get away with anything," says Gordon. "They've got to know who's boss—the sooner the better."

His WIN style carried over into an attempt to dominate the night-cook too. And as on his previous jobs, he was released before he upset the entire kitchen crew.

If I believe conflicts endanger a continuing relationship, I may give in rather than risk a confrontation. "I don't like it, but I'll swallow my own opinions just to keep the peace." This we call *Give in—to get along,* or YIELD.

Kathy hasn't a particularly dominating personality. She simply expresses her own opinions. But that's enough for Hal to feel that to contradict her will put their relationship in jeopardy. So, in spite of the strong person Hal seemed to be when they married, Kathy finds herself dominating their family decisions, and she doesn't like it. Because Hal fears that a conflict will shake their relationship, he YIELDS his own opinions whenever Kathy expresses hers.

"It isn't serious so far, just very frustrating. I *want* him to tell me what he wants—but if my desires are a little different, he backs off! I could cry—if it wouldn't make him feel awful!"

Perhaps it may be more important to me to give in to some of your demands in order to achieve some of my own. "I don't want you to win all the time, nor do I especially want to win over you always. In other words I don't want either one of us to be losers all the time." This is *Give a little—to win a little* or COMPROMISE.

Victor is teaching his third-year in social studies and his wife, Tricia, is completing a medical secretary's course at a junior college. Tricia would like very much to go on now and take some courses as a lab technician—but that means leaving the community. And it means Victor taking his chances in another school system—when a lot of teachers are out of work and competing hard for available jobs.

Whatever they decide to do—to stay or go—will test their relationship. If they go, Victor may need to take a nonteaching job which he won't find as fulfilling. If they stay, Tricia will give up her goals for the moment, and perhaps permanently. Their decision will be a COMPROMISE of wants and a readjustment in their relationship.

If conflict is an experience to grow by, for you and me both, then our differences aren't so much problem as possibility. "Conflicts are normal, and although the tensions and demands are fearsome at times, I know it is possible to work through our problems together." This is *Both sides win—if we resolve our differences,* or RE-SOLVE.

Golda's mother-in-law loved to give her grandchildren expensive gifts. Some of the gifts Golda felt were not good for her children, and her resentment deepened with each present—whether the gift was appropriate or not. Golda's frustration grew and she realized that to go on without doing something about it could only lead to a breakdown in her family relationships.

So the next time she visited with her mother-in-law, Golda opened the subject. "It took all my courage—and all the love I really have for her.

"She was angry at first—but then she began to see that I wasn't rejecting her, and that I really had a point about spoiling the children."

Golda and her mother-in-law negotiated a new arrangement. Now she brings smaller gifts of fruit the children like, and clothing they need. They RESOLVED a situation that threatened their relationship, and both are achieving their personal goals.

Now let's test your grasp of the five common styles of handling conflict.

In this situation, see if you can identify the styles Alex is considering to deal with his problem. Insert one of the following in the space provided for your answer:
WITHDRAW, WIN, YIELD, COMPROMISE, RE-SOLVE.

"He's stealing me blind," Alex says, numb with surprise. "Over two hundred dollars has come across the counter today, yet his cash totals show only a hundred twenty-four.

"But that's what you get for going into business with a

brother-in-law," Alex fumes to himself. "If that's the way he's going to be, I'll get out and he can have the whole business. I can do without this kind of hassle."

1. _____

After the initial shock, Alex began to ask himself some questions. "Maybe we can set up a better kind of partnership—so we can both get our hands in the cash register. He's not the only one who needs the money, that's for sure."

2. _____

Then his suspicions came down strong again and Alex sees no way but all-out-war.

"The miserable bum. I'll get him, and good. He's nothing but a crook, an embezzler! That's a criminal offense, and I'm calling the cops! He's got to learn he can't do this to me."

3. _____

Then Alex remembers his wife. "This is going to kill Wilma. Her own brother. Maybe for a while I'd better just forget it, to keep peace in the family. And watch the guy so he doesn't have the chance to do it so easy again."

4. _____

"At least I should talk with the guy first. Find out why he did it. Maybe he's got a money problem he hasn't wanted to talk about. Anyway we might have a chance of getting this straightened out."

5. _____

1. WITHDRAW. Alex doesn't want to face the tension of a confrontation. He infers this kind of thing is inevitable

and that he can't win anyway, so he wants out. His goals
suffer and so do his relationships.

2. COMPROMISE. Even if he bends his principles by accepting a lower ethical standard, he's willing to compromise. Personal goals and interpersonal relationships are
compromised. "You win a little, lose a little."

3. WIN. He is right; his brother-in-law is wrong. He
won't confuse the issue with any concern for interpersonal
relationships, so he secures his own personal position at all
costs.

4. YIELD. Relationships are more important than personal goals, so Alex considers giving in to a nasty situation
just to keep peace in the family.

5. RESOLVE. Finally Alex sees that he would really like
to save his personal integrity—and maybe his brother-in-
law's too—and restore their relationship. It won't be easy
for Alex or his wife or his brother-in-law, but working
through their situation will achieve a new relationship and
new goals for them all.

We often use others to help make headway in a fight.
(Some see the use of another person or persons as a sixth
style of conflict, although it can also be seen as part of the
"at all costs" strategy of the WIN style.)

Jesus of Nazareth found Himself in continuing conflict
with the religious leadership of Judea. It wasn't a conflict
of His choosing, but because He threatened their religion
He also threatened their self-image and lifestyle.

So as a strategy on one occasion they pulled an adul-
teress into their fight against Jesus. The account is found
in John 8:1-11 (author's paraphrase):

"Early next morning Jesus returned to the Temple and
all the people there gathered around him as he began to
teach. Then the scribes and the Pharisees brought in a
woman caught in adultery. They stood her before Jesus
and said, 'Teacher, this woman was caught in the very

act and in the Law, Moses said we are to stone such a woman to death. What do you say?'

"They did this as a trap to catch Jesus in some break with the Law, so they could charge him. . . .

"But Jesus responded, 'Let him among you who has never sinned throw the first stone at her. . . .'

"And when they heard what he said they went out one by one, leaving the woman standing there before Jesus.

"Then Jesus stood up and spoke to her. 'Where are they all? Has no one condemned you?'

"And she replied, 'No one, sir.'

" 'Neither do I condemn you,' said Jesus. 'Go home, and do not sin again.' "

The religious leaders were convinced Jesus was wrong, a lawbreaker and therefore a misleader of the people. Their method of dealing with Jesus was in the WIN style. They believed they were right. And they must win at all costs to save the people, the nation, the faith of their fathers, and their own beliefs. You can almost hear them thinking, "After all, how could I have been wrong all these years?"

In dealing with the situation Jesus did not *withdraw* from the confrontation, either physically or psychologically. Nor did He try to gain the respect of the leaders by *yielding* to their demands to stone the woman caught in the act of adultery. To do so might have set right His relationship with the priests and scribes—but He would have compromised His mission to redeem and set free those who needed Him most.

So He took the way of *resolution:* challenging the religious authorities to consider mercy along with their concern for law. Jesus pushed them to see that their motives were not after all a total concern for law and order because they too had failed the law. They too—like the rest of us—had sinned in their own way and fallen short of God's best for their lives.

Consider now several ways Jesus *might* have dealt with the woman after her accusers left, if He hadn't been who He was. Write in the appropriate style (*WITHDRAW, WIN, YIELD, COMPROMISE, RESOLVE*) to each of these and then check the style you think He actually used in the situation.

"Now that they're gone, let me tell you—if you don't cut this out I'll let them stone you the next time."

1. _____

"Your kind are always like this. I don't want anything to do with you. You go your way and I'll go mine."

2. _____

"If you'll try not to sin again, I might be able to help you."

3. _____

"I hope you don't mind what happened. After all, you have a right to your own point of view."

4. _____

"Neither do I condemn you. Go home and do not sin again."

5. _____

1. This is the WIN style similar to that of the religious

leaders who accused the woman. It sees standards as more important than persons.

2. This includes two of the identifying marks of the WITHDRAW style: the sense of inevitable defeat, and the action of rejection/withdrawal.

3. Bargaining tends to lower the standards of both parties in the COMPROMISE style.

4. Although Jesus did not condemn her, neither did He YIELD (as this style suggests) by trying to smooth over the situation.

5. This is of course exactly what Jesus said to her, as translated in The New English Bible. In the RESOLVE fashion, He upholds the highest personal goals the woman can achieve in urging her to live as God wants her to live. He has shown His love, both in defending her and in freeing her to make her own choices.

4
The Long View of Conflict

The five common styles of responding to conflict have been observed and defined in a series of tests by Telometrics International, of Conroe, Texas. Their observations have been verified in the clinical experiences of many phychiatrists, ministers, psychologists, and family counselors.

We might be tempted to think that these styles are relatively modern phenomena, linked to the twentieth century and our modern tensions. But it is a mistake to place such a burden on our times. The creativity of today's social scientists lies not so much in the discovery of conflict as in the analysis of its moods and in the channeling of its powers.

Conflict—like sex and poverty—has always been around. And so have the common styles of dealing with differences and the tensions they arouse. When Cain killed Abel in the dawn of history, he demonstrated a type of conflict as ancient as the first jealous blow and as modern as tomorrow's headlined family murder.

The story is recorded in Genesis 4. The first eleven chapters of the Bible are an intensely condensed record of the family history of mankind. It is a selective record detailing the spiritual devolution of humanity, from innocent fellowship with God to malevolent separation from Him and from each other.

The conflict between Cain and Abel has basic roots in the human personality and how we respond to our opportunities. Abel liked his job. Nothing about it seemed to disturb him. His work schedule suited his wife and his family. There were no in-law tensions. In fact, even God seemed to smile on Abel's life. (Or was it rather that the warmth of God's love was freely available to Abel because he wasn't blocking it from his life but was indeed living by faith?)

On the other hand, Cain didn't seem to think he was in the right occupation. He tried agribusiness but the profits were too low, or the days were too long, or he had to work too hard. "I mean, look at Abel's job," you can almost hear him thinking. "There's nothing to watching sheep. No grubbing in the ground, worrying about rain, or wondering when to harvest to receive the best prices.

"And God? What does He care? It looks like He's playing favorites with Abel anyway." So a root of bitterness sprouted, and instead of dealing with it in himself, Cain blamed his problem on his brother.

Jesus updated the story in his Sermon on the Mountain (Matthew 5 through 7). "You have learned that our forefathers were told, 'Do not commit murder; anyone who commits murder must be brought to judgement.' But what I tell you is this: Anyone who nurses anger against his brother must be brought to judgement" (Matthew 5:21, 22, NEB).

This first of many conflicts in the Bible aptly shows how far short we fall of our potential in relating to others. Cain's manufactured problems with Abel put him where we often find ourselves—in direct opposition to the first and greatest commandment of God. As Jesus expressed it, "You shall love the Lord your God with all your heart, and with all your soul, and with all your mind. This is the great and first commandment. And a second is like it, You shall love your neighbor as yourself" (Matthew 22:37-39, RSV).

Here is the classic statement of biblical conflict management: by faith we are to love God and act in love to our neighbors. As a practiced and practical discipline of living, this will develop within the individual the strength of character to rise above selfishness and deal justly and mercifully in conflict situations.

In later chapters we will further explore the influence of motives and feelings on the direction of a conflict.

> True or false: Conflicts and their management are a recent development of the social sciences.

> *Today's counselors have made great strides in helping people to understand and manage their conflicts, nevertheless the statement is false. The Bible records not only the presence of conflict but also the means of managing it through the development of a Christlike style of living by faith.*

Although conflict and the faith to deal with it are as ancient as mankind, modern skills of conflict management are tremendously helpful to faith. Even the reader who does not exercise faith will benefit by the methods now being employed by modern counselors. Nevertheless, it is when the wisdom of the age is enlightened by faith that it can benefit from the Wisdom of the Ages.

5
Which Style Is More Valuable?

As you might have expected, the five common styles can be seen in terms of their effectiveness in dealing with conflict—some more effective than others in certain situations. There are times when WIN is more useful than COMPROMISE. There are situations when the wisest and most loving action will be to YIELD to give the process of confrontation and negotiation a chance to work.

Nevertheless, we can generally say that RESOLVE is the ideal style. On a scale which measures concern for personal goals and relationships with others, the lowest value is given to WITHDRAW, the highest to RE-SOLVE, with the others ranged in between as shown below:

WITHDRAW
Lowest Value

Gives up on Goals and Relationship

When we withdraw from a conflict—either by walking out the door or by brooding in silence—we are at that time turning off the relationship. And also we are turning off any personal goals in that relationship. Unless used as a temporary cooling-off step toward RESOLVE it is wasteful. Because WITHDRAW gives up on both personal goals and on relationships, it should be considered the least helpful style for us in dealing with conflict.

WIN

Achieves Goals— Sacrifices Relationship

WIN is only slightly better in terms of value since, while gaining personal desires, it does so at the expense of relationships—and we assume that good relationships in a family or on the job are at least as important as personal desires!

YIELD

Maintains Relationship— Sacrifices Goals

YIELD has a higher value in terms of working toward a resolution of conflict—because it seeks to maintain the relationship, nevertheless it does so at the expense of personal goals of one of the parties.

COMPRO-MISE

Bargains Goals for Relationship

COMPROMISE at least seeks to work out some mutually bargained personal needs, but in doing so it threatens the relationship by compromising some basic values.

RESOLVE Highest Value	Works with Personal Goals to Improve Relationship	RESOLVE has the highest value because relationships are actually strengthened in the process of dealing most adequately with the conflict of personal needs.

Which style?

1. _____ Achieves personal goals at expense of relationships.

2. _____ Loses out on personal goals and relationships.

3. _____ Secures a high level of relationships while reaching for the most in personal needs

4. _____ Fails in personal needs while trying to keep relationships high.

5. _____ Bargains some needs for some cooperation in relationships.

1. WIN is not concerned with maintaining relationships, only in satisfying personal needs.

2. A person who WITHDRAWS from a conflict loses out on the opportunity for gaining personal goals within a relationship and turns away from the other person too.

3. If you are determined to RESOLVE a conflict you will be aiming for a high level in relationships while still working out your own needs, as well as those of the other person.

4. You may find that in order to preserve a relationship with another, you feel it necessary to YIELD your own personal desires.

5. *COMPROMISE chooses to negotiate different needs in a middle ground of relationships.*

Given the value of relationships and the scale of priorities we have assigned to them we can look at the methods of dealing with conflict in an ideal ladder of value like this:

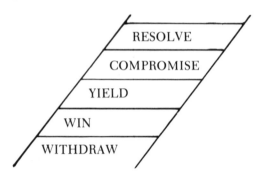

Social scientists have tested many thousands of persons in researching this approach to conflict. They have found that most people at one time or another use each of the styles on the ladder, but not necessarily in the order shown. Remember, even the person who consistently uses the RESOLVE style will find good reason to WITHDRAW on occasion.

When we are faced with conflict we respond with one of these styles as our usual or typical response. If that doesn't work, we shift to our next preference. This shift is done almost without thinking, and we may shift through all styles in an order of preference to which we have become accustomed.

Some persons, because of the way their parents handled their differences, choose another ladder arrangement than the ideal of RESOLVE, COMPROMISE, YIELD, WIN, WITHDRAW. A WIN dominant father may influence his sons to follow a ladder of preferred responses similar to his own.

The wife of the WIN dominant husband is likely to develop YIELD as her typical response since she may find it too threatening to their relationship to try to COMPROMISE, for instance.

You have developed your own ladder of response because of several factors:

1. As a child, you observed and were influenced by your parents' styles, and the styles of others closest to you.

2. In developing your personality, you accepted or rejected the style preference of those models closest to you.

3. As you became more independent of your family in school, you likely modified your response ladder to include the influences of your peers.

4. The pressures of society in general, especially your work environment and your intimate relationships, have solidified your present preference of responses.

5. Yet in spite of your trained or typical response you have become aware that it may be possible for you to react in different ways at different times and to choose your reaction style.

True or False? There is only one way people respond to conflict.

There are at least five identifiable styles and these five may be arranged in many different sequences or preferences (ladders) of response. The statement is false.

Check the possible influences which shape a typical style preference:

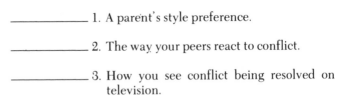

_____ 1. A parent's style preference.

_____ 2. The way your peers react to conflict.

_____ 3. How you see conflict being resolved on television.

You are correct if you checked all of the above as influences which shape a style preference. We are influenced by what we observe in our parents, our peers, and by how society resolves its conflicts, even as portrayed on television.

True or False? Most people use each of the styles of conflict response at one time or another.

If you answered true you are correct. All five of these styles are useful to us under certain circumstances.

Consider for example the various ways Jesus responded to the persons who confronted Him. He too was free to use any of the styles to suit the situation.

When we study Jesus' life, it is important to remind ourselves that each of His actions were a part of a larger purpose involving people. Throughout history Jesus has been held in high regard by non-Christians because of the clear insights He expressed about human nature. However, Christians acknowledge that Jesus' purpose was more than to show us what we are like. The Bible describes centuries of conflict as humanity consistently rejected God through rejecting His call, choosing our own way of life rather than His.

Yet even Jesus, whose greatest purpose was to RESOLVE the conflict between man and God often used WITHDRAW, YIELD, WIN, and COMPROMISE styles within His larger goal. Take a look at the following situations as the Bible records them. What style do you believe Jesus was using in each instance? (This brief section is for personal exploration and will not be followed by questions and answers.)

Wherever Jesus went crowds soon collected. As His influence widened, the religious leaders (who were also politically responsible to Roman authorities) sought to discredit Him to the people. But Jesus debated with them, confronting their traditional arguments with biblical authorities from His own study. In one situation "Jesus was approached by a group of Pharisees and lawyers from Jerusalem, with the question: 'Why do your disciples break the ancient tradition? They do not wash their hands before meals.' He answered them: 'And what of you? Why do you break God's commandment in the interest of your tradition? For God said, "Honour your father and mother," and, "The man who curses his father or mother must suffer death." But you say, "If a man says to his father or mother, 'Anything of mine which might have been used for your benefit is set apart for God,' then he must not honour his father or his mother." You have made God's law null and void out of respect for your tradition. What hypocrisy! Isaiah was right when he prophesied about you: 'This people pays me lipservice, but their heart is far from me; their worship of me is in vain, for they teach as doctrines the commandments of men' '' (setting: Matthew 15:1-20, NEB).

But neither His biblical reasoning nor the remarkable works that He did among the people convinced the leaders that Jesus was their long-awaited Messiah-Christ. Instead they sought to kill Him for this blasphemous claim. Later Jesus deliberately exposed himself to their conspiracies. But He preferred to choose His own time to go up to them in Jerusalem. So until He was ready for that confrontation He took His disciples and withdrew into the wilderness. "Accordingly Jesus no longer went about publicly in Judaea, but left that region for the country bordering on the desert, and came to a town called Ephraim, where he stayed with his disciples" (setting: John 11:45-57, NEB).

When Jesus did come to Jerusalem His actions against the sacrifice-sellers and money-exchangers jolted everyone. "And he . . . began to drive out those who sold and those who bought in the temple . . . and said to them 'Is it not written, "My house shall be called a house of prayer for all nations"? But you have made it a den of robbers' " (setting: Mark 11:11-19, RSV). What style is he using here?

Yet at His arrest, during His interrogation, throughout His trial, in the lashing He received, and through the terrible hours of His execution, Jesus chose to yield to the purposes of His persecutors. He absorbed their hostility, and in the end spoke back the word of forgiveness, grace, and acceptance. "And Jesus said, 'Father, forgive them; for they know not what they do' " (setting: Luke 23:18-49, RSV).

Now let's explore how you handle conflict, and see how you are doing so far in *When You Don't Agree*.

6
Analyze Your Progress

What is your typical response? What is the preference ladder you choose to use? It is helpful to know how you normally react now so that you can see clearly the directions in which you prefer to go.

The following paragraphs describe in broader terms the characteristics of the five styles you have studied previously. Choose the one which seems to be least like the way you usually react and give it a value of 1. Then choose the style most useful to you, and give it a value of 5. Arrange the balance of your value ladder as honestly as you can.

WITHDRAW. Conflict is one of the necessary evils in human affairs. Because most people are more concerned about themselves, conflict just means a frustrating and punishing drain on my emotional energies. I'm not going to succeed in changing anything and may make things worse. Even if I did get involved I'm not the kind to win, so I prefer to back off. Silence and noncommitment and a little distance from others can serve me best in handling conflicts.

I value this style _____

WIN. In conflicts as in life it's the survival of the fittest, and I believe right prevails. The truth for me can only be lived by strength of character and unswerving dedication to the goals established for my life. Consequently, in conflict with persons whose opinions, ideals and goals are in doubt, I owe it to myself and those who rely on my judgment to prevail and win clearly. To be wishy-washy is to fail, because by weakness in preserving a relationship, truth and honor may be threatened. Therefore, I will persuade and coerce and use all the methods most people accept in order to achieve what I believe in.

I value this style _____

YIELD. I think conflicts can be very hard on relationships, particularly if I let a situation get out of hand. When someone differs from me I can easily feel rejected, and I think others really feel that way too if they would admit it. That's why I think open conflicts must be avoided, and this often calls for a willingness to give up my own interests for the sake of a continuing relationship. Even if it means cooperation in spite of my own opinions, I avoid a confrontation. It's better to look for the good in others than risk disruption of the relationship.

I value this style _____

COMPROMISE. This one is hard for me to recognize in myself because it's so much like life—it's never possible for everyone to be satisfied. The best chance we have is to try and achieve the best for the most of us. At times that means giving in on some things to keep my relationships in reasonable shape. In an open conflict I like to get things smoothed over as best as possible, and that often takes all the negotiating ability I've got. And even though that may mean bending things around and compromising our values, at least we can move ahead together.

I value this style _____

RESOLVE. I can't be satisfied with just letting things go, or settling for less than the best that we can work out together. If I express my feelings and my needs clearly without trying to pull the other person down, and if I can help others in the conflict to do the same, then we don't need to feel personally wounded. And if we work at our differences properly we will resolve them in a way that often opens up new possibilities for us we never saw before. I'm not afraid of conflict because it can have so many good results for our relationships in the process of solving our problems.

I value this style _____

Don't despair if your conflict response ladder seems to be the opposite of the ideal—at least you know where you are! And you now know the direction you need to work to improve your relationships and the achievement of personal goals.

Now before we go on to Part II let's take an overview of Part I as a whole.

Theresa and Raymond are getting a divorce. They've been married eight years and both come from families where relationships were reasonably stable and happy. While she is sure divorce is the only answer to an incompatible situation, Theresa blames herself for failure.

"If I had stood up to Ray from the beginning," she told the marriage counselor, "we wouldn't have got into the cycle we did. But he would insist on his way, and I'd give in just to keep the peace."

From Theresa's story, what style did Raymond generally use in their conflicts? _____
What style did Theresa see herself using? _____

Raymond seems to use the WIN style on Theresa. And she would YIELD to preserve the relationship.

Raymond was persuaded to join Theresa in her next counseling session. It was soon obvious to the counselor that Ray, when challenged, tended to shrug off the situation and refuse to talk.

On the other hand, Theresa, sensing what was happening, began to offer excuses for Ray's behavior to the counselor.

"I've already had a session with you," Theresa pointed out, "and Ray hasn't. Why don't you explain to him what he might be doing."

Then she turned to her husband, "I won't talk anymore, Ray. Please listen to what he says about handling conflicts."

Check which of the following you think Raymond is using here:
_____ a. WIN
_____ b. WITHDRAW

Check which style you believe Theresa is now using:
_____ a. COMPROMISE
_____ b. YIELD

As Raymond refuses to talk he is withdrawing from the conflict, while Theresa shows some bargaining skills. If you checked (b) for Ray and (a) for Theresa you are correct.

Theresa's ladder of style begins with YIELD. When pushed she comes back with a desire to fight for relationships, using the COMPROMISE style.

Ray's WIN style isn't strong on relationships to begin with and his move to using WITHDRAW isn't surprising.

After several sessions of counsel, both Raymond and Theresa began working toward the ideal ladder, and the counselor has urged them to reconsider their divorce action.

Arrange the five styles in their *ideal* or most appropriate ladder for handling conflicts, by ranking them 5, most ideal, 4, next most ideal, and so on down to 1, least useful in resolving conflict.

____ COMPROMISE   ____ YIELD   ____ WIN
____ WITHDRAW   ____ RESOLVE

The ladder of style which is held to be most appropriate in resolving conflict is

> 5—RESOLVE, most useful
> 4—COMPROMISE
>   3—YIELD
>   2—WIN
>   1—WITHDRAW, least useful

True or false? It is possible to change the way we respond to differences.

This is true, not only from the standpoint of making a conscious selection of how we respond, but also in our habitual reactions.

As a final two-stage exercise, think about one specific conflict you faced recently, in your family perhaps or in your work. Try to remember the feelings you had about the other person or persons involved.

What did you do with those feelings? How did you react? Did what you say help to resolve your differences? What did you do with your voice and your gestures? How did the other person's responses affect you?

If you wish, use the space below to describe in a few sentences the actions you took and the feelings you experienced in an explanation of the style or combination of styles you employed.

Now compare your statement with the previous descriptions of WITHDRAW, WIN, YIELD, COM- PROMISE, RESOLVE. What could you have done to re- solve the conflict, knowing what you know now? If you wish, outline the steps you would take in a similar situa- tion with a few sentences in the space following:

7
In Hope of Change

No matter how we have lived in the past, we can learn new habits. And we can draw upon the power of God to help us transform our deepest reactions. This is precisely what Christianity is all about. With the help of Christ we *can* turn from styles of response that frustrate the highest love and the highest aim for our lives. We *can* develop new ways of dealing with conflict and find the inner strength to carry through with our best intentions.

And that is why this chapter is here, and closes Part I without any questions except the ones you may come up with as you read.

The Bible holds up the personality of Jesus as the living-among-us evidence of what God is like. "He is the image of the invisible God. . . . For in him the complete being of God, by God's own choice, came to dwell" (Colossians 1:15-20, NEB). He is also the living model of what we can be, *with the strength of the Spirit of God to bring this about.* "I can do all things through Christ which strengtheneth me" (Philippians 4:13, KJV).

It won't be easy. For many of us the way we handle conflicts has hardened into grooves that have become a part of us. And to change is devastating. Because of this, we may back away from change, preferring the comfort of our grooves until the agony of unresolved conflict drives us to the desire for change again. We may even have tried to change a number of times and failed, adding the pain of helplessness to our dilemma.

Yet is must be repeated: *we can change.* It may take a longer time than we want God to use. But if our responses to conflict are deeply grooved, we may need to work with our faith for a time, practice our love, and enter into the lifelong experience of being "discipled" by Christ. After all, it took time to get us where we are now. It is only reasonable to expect some length of time for God to shift us from our present style and establish us in a new pattern of living.

If we are impatient, God is not. He is infinitely patient with us. He is even quicker to forgive us than we are to ask His forgiveness. And His forgiving is aimed at reconciling us in all our relationships with all of the others—the neighbors—of our lives. And that is why the Great Commandment of God includes our neighbor: "Thou shalt love the Lord your God with all your heart, with all your soul, with all your strength, *and your neighbor as yourself.*"

Let's say it again in a different way: our personal responses to conflict can be improved and made manageable. If that seems impossible, God can and does do remarkable things for us through the enabling help of His Spirit—*if we are willing to be helped.*

"If you really love me, you will keep the commandments I have given you and I shall ask the Father to give you someone else to stand by you, to be with you always. I mean the Spirit of Truth, whom the world cannot accept, for it can neither see nor recognize that Spirit. But you recognize him for he is with you now and will be in your hearts. I am not going to leave you alone in the world—I am coming to you. In a very little while, the world will see me no more but you will see me, because I am really alive and you will be alive too. When that day comes, you will realize that I am in my Father, that you are in me, and I am in you" (John 14:15-20, Phillips).

"But if all it takes to resolve conflicts is to become a Christian, then why do so many Christians continue to have conflicts?" The question is legitimate, and if you haven't asked it, perhaps you should.

It is tempting to hope for a simple solution to our problems. We'd like to be able to wave a magic wand or pray a prayer and wake up in a new situation. It would be pleasant if "Jesus is the answer" could become our password into the land of the trouble-free.

But becoming a Christian is only the beginning of possibilities for us. Behind the scenes in the new Christian, a lot of theological realignments have taken place, as several writers of the New Testament point out. The significance of these doctrinal explanations is that, having said "yes" to God, we have put ourselves in the position of being open and available to change. *Or at least in as many areas of our lives as we choose to be open and available for such change.*

The power of God to bring about change is documentable. If a group of social scientists were to interview a broad sample of Christians, they would find a repeated—and repeatable—theme: "God gave grace (or power) which enabled a positive change in my life."

But it would also be found that many of the same persons could list areas in their lives where needed change has not yet happened. Furthermore, if spouses or friends were invited to list needed changes in these same Christians, their lists might be quite different from the persons' own list. We do not always know ourselves as others do. And until we begin to see ourselves more clearly we may be unable to recognize the need for change in areas that are clear to others.

That's why Christians need to learn conflict resolution skills also. Because in the process of learning, we will discover things about ourselves. And again we will face the choice of being open and available for change. The power of God will be there to help, but it is in the nature of God—and this is highly visible in Jesus—not to force anything upon us we do not choose for ourselves.

For those who are not yet persuaded of a transcending power from God, let me say two more things. First, a new, changed life is central to the hope which Christianity has claimed since its inception. This new life is not achieved through rules to be followed (although laws are necessary for those who will not be ruled otherwise). Nor is it attained through a religion dramatized by shaved heads or austere clothing and similar sacred cows.

No, the Christian "way" so frequently referred to in the New Testament is the way of transformation by the presence of "Christ in you, the hope of glory," as the Apostle Paul described it to the Colossian Christians (Colossians 1:27).

It is a proven way insofar as it has been demonstrated in the lives of Christians down through the centuries. Believing God and applying themselves to following Christ by faith, they know in their own lives how much has been changed. If the transformation has not been complete or perfect (as the world seems to expect from all those who break with its practicing of unbelief), nevertheless it has been significant to those who have been changed.

This brings us to the second consideration, the ancient accusation by unbelievers that "there are too many hypocrites in the church." It is as if the person enjoying his unbelief is judging the Christian for what he has not yet attained—his lack of perfection. Instead, the Christian asks to be measured—if measured he must be—by how much his life has been transformed *from what it was*.

There's a saying, "Be patient, God's not finished with me yet." Life is a process, a movement, and nothing about it is static. What we are is largely a result of our past responses, what we will become begins with our responses to the possibilities coming at us now.

We may feel locked into our present way of life and be unhappy about it. Or we may be quite satisfied with our life now and happy with the direction it is going.

In either case, change is a reality that must be reckoned with. As surely as tomorrow will come, tomorrow's circumstances will bring new situations demanding your response. If you choose to be guided and helped by the Spirit of God in how you respond, then your responses—whether the situations appear to be good or bad—will be healthy and your character will mature in the best possible direction.

"If you are then 'risen' with Christ, reach out for the highest gifts of Heaven, where your master reigns in power. Give your heart to the heavenly things, not to the passing things of earth. For, as far as this world is concerned, you are already dead, and your true life is a hidden one in Christ. One day, Christ, the secret center of our lives, will show himself openly, and you will all share in that magnificent dénouement.

"In so far, then, as you have to live upon this earth, consider yourselves dead to worldly contacts: have nothing to do with sexual immorality, dirty-mindedness, uncontrolled passion, evil desire, and the lust for other people's goods, which last, remember, is as serious a sin as idolatry. It is because of these very things that the holy anger of God falls upon those who refuse to obey him. And never forget that you had your part in those dreadful things when you lived that old life.

"But now, put all these things behind you. No more evil temper or furious rage: no more evil thoughts or words about others, no more evil thoughts or words about God, and no more filthy conversation. Don't tell one another lies anymore, for you have finished with the old man and all he did and have begun life as the new man, who is out to learn what he ought to be, according to the plan of God. In this new man of God's design there is no distinction between Greek and Hebrew, Jew or Gentile, foreigner or savage, slave or free man. Christ is all that matters, for Christ lives in them all" (Colossians 3:1-11, Phillips).

Part II
Improving Communication Skills

8
Some Problems in Speaking

I am listening to my own hurts so hard I can't hear what you're saying.

Frank's frustration is obvious in his voice. "She knows what I'm going to say before I open my mouth. So I'm on the defensive, and I want to say a half-dozen different things quick before she tells me what I'm really thinking."

On two occasions Frank physically abused his wife and this is a deep embarrassment to him. "But she gets me so fired up by confusing what I say into what she wants to hear that I lose control of myself."

Frank's anger is turned in on himself as much as it is directed at his wife. He's ashamed of his inability to communicate his thoughts and feelings. He despises the slow and arduous way he seems to take in connecting his thoughts and his words.

In any conflict it's necessary to communicate clearly what you mean by your words and acts so that the other person can understand where you are.

Similarly, if you are to grasp what the other person is

saying or doing, you will want to understand his meanings as well as his acts and words.

At the end of this section you should be able to chart for yourself a working explanation of the process of communication.

Also you will have had the opportunity to test a number of your own problems of listening accurately and speaking clearly against the common experiences of many others in our society.

Finally you will have explored and practiced five skills for clear projecting/speaking and six perceiving/ listening skills.

What is involved in the process of communication? Hearing. Gestures. Speech. And thought. One of the sources of problems in communication is the difference in the speed of speech and thought.

Thinking speed is believed to be around 400 words per minute. Radio and television news announcers speak at about 170 words a minute. But they are only able to speak this quickly because they are reading from prepared scripts. The rest of us have to plod along at around 100 words a minute, including the "ums" and "ahs" and other fillers we use while we translate thoughts and ideas into words. And because we think faster than the person we are listening to can speak, we may fall into the habit of anticipating what the speaker is going to say, rightly or wrongly. Or we may simply drift off into thoughts of our own choosing.

Speaking isn't an easy process. Most of us find it difficult to express ourselves clearly.

We find it reasonably easy to describe simple *facts or*

objects. "The fruit is round" communicates one fact about the fruit—particularly if we can use our hands to help show just how round it is. That's why we'll be using the term *projecting* to include gestures and emotional levels as well as speech.

"It's bigger than an apple, about the size of a softball" will describe the fruit more clearly, if the listener is familiar with the size of a softball. "When cut in half the fruit has sections like an orange" should begin to project the idea of a grapefruit to the listener.

Now while describing the physical characteristics may be relatively simple, think of describing the process of making the fruit into juice. Even the most primitive squeezing by hand can begin to sound complicated.

That is why *processes* and *events* are more difficult to explain clearly without straining our capacity to select words and gestures.

"Hold half of the fruit over a jar and begin to squeeze it with both hands so the juice goes into the jar. It tastes like an orange, but not as sweet."

But wait! Now we are moving beyond facts and processes to concepts and opinions. What is sweet? Not as sweet? How sweet?

Some grapefruits are sweeter than some oranges— which is a *concept or opinion* many orange eaters will agree with, but only because they have themselves tasted a sweet grapefruit and a tart orange. (What is tart?)

Facts are relatively simple to communicate about with clarity.

Processes and events are somewhat more difficult to discuss.

Concepts, opinions, and emotions give us the most trouble in communicating.

Fill in the blanks with the right numbers.

(1) Thinking speed is believed to be _____ words a minute, while

(2) Talking speed is around _____ words a minute.

a. 1000	e. 800
b. 200	f. 100
c. 650	g. 50
d. 400	h. 320

Thinking speed is (d) 400 words a minute. Speaking speed is around 100 words a minute (f).

The difference in thinking and talking speeds can create which (one or more) of the following problems for a listener?

_____ a. Listener's thoughts can go on into other distracting channels.

_____ b. Listener can incorrectly anticipate what the speaker is going to say.

_____ c. Listener can search his experience for possible meanings to check with the speaker.

Both (a) and (b) are definite problems for a listener which can contribute to misunderstanding. If the listener is prepared to check out the alternate possibilities of meaning with the speaker as in (c), this is not a problem but a definite asset to achieving understanding. This is one of the perceiving skills we will be exploring further in Part II.

Classify the statements below by filling in the blanks with one of the following:

a. Fact

b. Event or process

c. Concept, opinion, or emotion

_____ 1. "You know, Ruth, this will be the first weekend we can do what we want together for two months.

_____ 2. "Then your mother called. And when I told her we were going camping, she got your dad on the phone. Between the two of them they arranged it so we should come up there instead.

_____ 3. "Your folks are always doing that, every time. They seem to know just the right moment to foul things up."

The first is a statement of fact (a). The second is a description of the conversation and what went on during the discussion (b), a process, or event. In 3, emotions begin to surface and an opinion is stated (c).

Communicating our thoughts clearly can be very frustrating. It involves more than the selection of words, because words are only part of the whole process of projecting a meaning. And what we mean to express may not be completely clear even to us. Our minds race ahead of our tongues and what we say is often only part of what we mean to project.

No wonder we can be misunderstood!

9
Meanings Are Inside

When you speak, your meaning or intention is in your mind and only partially expressed in your words. At best, your words only sketch a picture of what you mean. At worst, what you say projects the wrong picture entirely and your meaning is lost.

Yet we persist in believing that words in themselves hold all meaning, and all that is necessary is to look in a dictionary, check the definition listed, and we shall know exactly what the person meant who used the word. We forget that dictionaries merely collect common meanings that people give to words.

But words do not "mean." Words are only conveyers of *some* of the meaning or intention given them by the person using them.

When a person uses a word, he alone gives it meaning. His meaning may resemble the common meanings of the word in the community—or it may not. Whatever is said, the full meaning remains somewhere inside the person's mind and spirit. When you speak to me, I can only infer what you mean; I cannot be certain unless I check my inferences with you. And this may take a little more time than we're used to giving!

"Meanings are in people," to use the memorable words of David K. Berlo, chairman of the department of communication arts at Michigan State University. Meanings are personal, our own property. They are complete in us, and only partly revealed in our messages.

We are lazy. We'd prefer to have meanings limited to a simple definition in a word spoken or a truth written or a law recorded. It would save us the hard work of digging behind the words for understanding. And we prefer the security of fixed meanings to the insecurity of meaning hidden in the person who speaks or writes or records.

This was a continuing problem for many of the religious leaders who found Jesus so hard to pin down. The Pharisees and scribes (law interpreters) in particular were frustrated with Jesus. They were accustomed to precise meaning in the word of the law and avoided the meaning God intended by the words. They had become familiar with the letter of the law rather than its spirit. For instance, they objected to Jesus' interpretations of the food laws. "Some of the scribes and Pharisees from Jerusalem came and asked Jesus, 'Why do your disciples break our ancient tradition and eat their food without washing their hands properly first? . . .'

"Then [Jesus] . . . called the crowd to him and said, 'Listen, and understand this thoroughly! It is not what goes *into* a man's mouth that makes him common or unclean. It is what comes *out* of a man's mouth that makes him unclean. . . .'

"Don't you see that whatever goes *into* the mouth passes into the stomach and then out of the body altogether? But the things that come *out* of a man's mouth come from his heart and mind, and it is they that really make a man unclean. For it is from a man's mind that evil thoughts arise—murder, adultery, lust, theft, perjury and blasphemy. These are the things which make a man unclean, not eating without washing his hands properly' " (Matthew 15:1-20, Phillips).

The Pharisees were angry that a tradition had been broken by Jesus' disciples. But Jesus challenged them to consider the meaning behind the words of the law they were imposing. The interpretation of the Pharisees declared that a person was "unclean" who ate with unwashed hands, and thus the person became subject to being corrected and ceremonially reestablished.

Instead of accepting the Pharisees rigid and superficial meaning of "unclean," Jesus reached for the spirit of the tradition. In a similar situation He accused the Pharisees of cleaning the outside of the cup rather than the inside, of making outward appearance more important than inward reality. A modern parallel to Jesus' response might be, "A person is honest not because he makes himself look honest to other people but because he is so in his personality and in his actions."

Check the correct statement(s):
_____ a. Meanings are in the messages people give.
_____ b. A good place to check the final meaning of a word is in the dictionary.
_____ c. Meanings for a word or a message are only what people intend them to mean.
_____ d. I think I know what I mean, but I can only infer what you mean.

Response (a) is incorrect because a message can be interpreted different ways by different people. The only correct interpretation or meaning rests with the person who gave the message.

Response (b) is also incorrect because, while a dictionary is a good place to find what many people use a word to mean, the final meaning nevertheless remains with whoever uses the word and gives it his own meaning at that moment. And that is why (c) is correct.

Response (d) is also correct. Because we can only infer what another person means, we are apt to misunderstand the message. Nevertheless, we can work at achieving understanding by learning and using listening or perceiving skills.

10
Sending and Perceiving
a Message

When we have something to say, we open our mouths and say it. Or at least we try. What goes on when we try to project a message? Let's take the process apart in several steps:

Intended Message
1. You intend to say something.

Message Equipment
2. You select some equipment by which to ship the message from your storehouse of communicating tools:

a. *Words:* ones familiar to you from an accumulated vocabulary and with your own understanding of their meanings.

b. *Drives:* a select amount of motivating steam, excitement, anger, love, amusement, scorn, etc., with which to unite your word meanings and your emotional state.

c. *Expressions:* gestures of face, hands, body, and tone of voice to emphasize and give a framework for your words and drives.

Sending Method

3. You then put together this package of meaning and project it through a method that is uniquely your own, arising from your background and experiences.

Some persons project their messages quickly, with many elaborate gestures, as it may have been done in their family or neighborhood for generations.

Some people with limited vocabularies develop a projecting shorthand that is difficult to comprehend and we have to depend much on their drives and expressions for understanding.

While some project anger with shouts, I personally tend to speak more quietly than usual, and more intently. Unless you were familiar with my sending system, you might underestimate my emotional communication and misunderstand my words.

Let's diagram this part of the process:

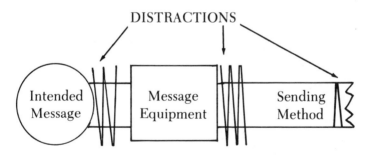

The up-and-down zig-zags in the diagram represent those complicating distractions that interfere with the projecting process: It is a hot humid day. A radio nearby is playing a familiar song. Some interrupted work lies waiting. And a word that suits just won't come to mind so another is substituted that doesn't project meaning quite as appropriately.

Anger, scorn, pity, excitement, and love are elements of which of the following parts of the sending or projecting diagram?

_____ a. Sending method
_____ b. Message equipment
_____ c. Intended message

The emotional drives we experience as we project a message are tools we use to help make our meaning clear, so (b) is correct.

Now let's look at how I perceive your message. Note that it is in the reverse order:

Perceiving Method

1. I have developed over the years a method of receiving and interpreting messages that is uniquely my own just as you have yours. I've often found myself trying to finish the speaker's sentences, attempting to leapfrog the words to get at the message. Some others I know have developed a distaste for excitable people, or are impatient with shy, quiet speakers.

Many of us do something while the other is talking: write a note to ourselves, start a household chore, simply stand up and walk around. Not all of us will do so for the same reasons. One might pace the room, impatient with the gap in thinking and speaking speeds. Another may be trying through "body language" to get a word in edgewise. Still others may prefer to be easily distracted rather than to work at listening.

And if you are like most of us, your perceiving system will begin to interpret the message almost before it gets to you. Yet there are those who have trained themselves to wait for the complete message, who concentrate their attention on the other's meanings behind the words and gestures and drives.

Message Equipment

2. Having channeled your message through my perceiving method, I'll now take it apart with my message equipment. But the meanings won't be yours entirely; much will be my own.

a. *Expressions.* Certain gestures and body positions have a usual meaning to me and that's how I will interpret yours, even though that may not be what you mean by the gesture. Tears in your eyes may only speak weakness to some people, whether or not your emotional drive and your words express anger or joy or compassion.

b. *Drive.* I tend to respond to quiet, unemotional speech with inattention, even boredom. We respond to each other's feelings in different ways, irrespective of the meaning behind the feelings.

c. *Words.* I filter the words you speak through my own vocabulary. Influenced by my perceiving method and my evaluation of your expressions and drive, I will select those meanings I believe are appropriate.

Interpreted Message

3. The message and meaning I put together is a combination of what you have projected and what I have perceived. It may be very close to the intended message—yet often it is not.

Note the distractions in perceiving as well. The job

waiting for me to do, a car going by, an uncomfortable chair, even the way the person who is speaking turns a pencil as he talks may be distracting.

DISTRACTIONS

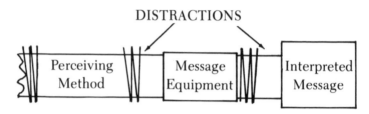

True or false? Your sending method is the unique way you receive and interpret messages.

Sorry if this turns out to be a trick question for you. This is the way we described the perceiving method. If you checked true, which is incorrect, you may simply have experienced one of those common mishaps in communication, reading into the question what you expected, thinking "perceiving" while you read "sending."

In the diagram of the process of communicating we have studied, try to place the following words in the appropriate blanks.

a. Perceiving method   d. Interpreted Message
b. Intended Message   e. Message Equipment
c. Distractions   f. Sending Method

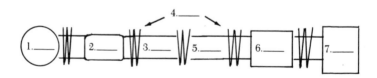

1. b,   2. e,   3. f,   4. c,   5. a,   6. e,   7. d.

In the space below, list at least five distractions which interfere with communications.

Many items could be listed, so consider your answers correct if they included among others physical distractions such as interruptions, noises, discomfort; and mental distractions such as boredom, job, pressures, even wandering thoughts caused by something said or done by the speaker.

Now that we have looked at the process of sending and perceiving a message, let's start with the first part of the process and try to improve our sending skills.

11
Improving Your Sending Skills

Saying plainly and clearly what we mean is not simply choosing the proper words. Word selection is a relatively minor member of the team of five sending or projecting skills:

1. Integrate yourself with your message.
2. Avoid questions that are not questions.
3. Select specific words and statements the other can understand.
4. Speak with respect for your listener.
5. Check your message with the listener.

Skill 1: Integrate yourself with your message.

We usually think of skills in terms of something we do: the carpenter, the surgeon, the artist. But the artisan becomes noted for what he or she does only when the skills of the craft become a part of the personality. So in that sense what we do is also what we are. And that is the basis of integrity.

However, in our modern sophisticated world much that we say to each other is not what we are really thinking. We describe that kind of pragmatic communicating by a number of phrases—political hyperbole, tact, white lies, and several other descriptions which we choose not to print.

We are used to television and radio commercials and the subtleties of advertising. A national bakery infers it bakes "natural" bread by saying it wraps its loaves "naturally." We are told by politicians what is needed to secure our votes. In fact we are apt to vote for an "image" that bears little resemblance to the person behind the publicity.

Who is real? The image or the person on the level under the image who tells you who he is? Or is there another level under the words where the thoughts and intentions work?

We tend to become multilevel people—one level hidden deep inside, another for friends and associates, a third for the public, perhaps another for the people we work with. Is it any wonder our messages aren't clear when we hardly know who we are ourselves?

When we get into a conflict we are even more apt to hide behind our defenses. We say no when we mean yes, yes when we mean maybe, and maybe when we mean "drop dead."

Jesus confronts that kind of multilevel personality: "Whatever you have to say let your 'yes' be a plain 'yes' and your 'no' be a plain 'no'—anything more than this has a taint of evil" (Matthew 5:37, Phillips).

The heart of Christian realism is becoming an integrated, single-level person. No masks or images—just *you*—open to yourself and to God. And willing by faith to grow, as He helps you grow, into your full potential as a child of God. That's essential Christianity; no more and no less.

So the first skill in projecting a clear understanding

message is to become a clearly understandable personality. Then your messages are you. There is no hidden you to muddy up the clear water of your message.

One place to begin is to avoid exaggeration. Use fewer adjectives. Practice clear, single-level speech. Drop any pretenses of knowing things you only guess, of being better informed or more certain of facts than you actually are.

Speaking as an integrated single-level person calls for which (one or more) of the following:

_____ a. Choosing your words carefully so as not to expose what you are thinking.

_____ b. Integrating your thoughts and emotions with what you are saying.

_____ c. Becoming an integrated whole person by faith in Jesus Christ.

Single-level speaking is the opposite to the two-level answer given in (a), which is incorrect. The first skill in projecting a clear message is to pull together underlying motives, thoughts, and emotions with projecting speech and actions, thus (b) is correct. And as most people soon discover, integrating the several different persons each of us seem to be takes an ability to be whole and wholesome that we can't quite get ahold of ourselves. At least not consistently.

And that is the basic problem in all human relationships. We are not what we could be, or should be. As the Apostle Paul put it, "I often find that I have the will to do good, but not the power. That is, I don't accomplish the good I set out to do, and the evil I don't really want to do I find I am always doing. . . . It is an agonizing situation, and who on earth can set me free from the clutches of my own sinful nature? I thank God there is a way out through Jesus Christ our Lord" (Romans 7:18-25, Phillips).

Becoming an integrated whole person through faith in

Jesus Christ is the first step in the right direction. The love and grace of God can then become available to begin a faith-continuing string of victories over self-defeating attitudes. He has the strength to help you be honest with yourself—and others—when you are least likely to be, in a conflict with someone important to you. And even a slip back into failure need be no more than an incident because God's forgiving mercy and renewing grace will continue to be available.

Skill 2: Avoid questions that are not questions.

"Why don't you want to try and understand me?"

"When are you ever going to do what I ask you to do?"

Remember when you were asked "questions" like these—and you wanted to cry or run or hitback in some way? These are questions that are really traps, put downs, demands to straighten up or else.

If you ask your wife, "Why don't you want to try and understand me?" you aren't looking for information as with a real question. This actually is an accusation designed to put blame on the listener. You are inferring that she (1) does not understand, (2) won't even try, and (3) has a hidden and unworthy motive.

If you ask your son, "When are you ever going to do what I ask you to do?" you are saying (1) he never does anything right, (2) you doubt if he ever will, and (3) he better change to suit you.

"Questions that aren't" are confusing at best, irritating and frustrating at their usual worst.

1. *The Leading Question* attempts to limit or restrict the possible responses of the other person, and leads him in the direction you want him to go.

"Don't you think that . . .?"

"Isn't it true that . . .?"

"Wouldn't you rather . . .?"

2. *The Punishing Question* challenges the other person's opinions, rights, even his intelligence and punishes him for his views.

"Why did you say . . .?"

"Why didn't you try . . .?"

3. *The Hypothetical Question* is used to criticize another's situation or action by suggesting your own "better" point of view.

"If you were running this, wouldn't you rather . . .?"

4. *The Command Question* demands action in the form of a question.

"When are you going to . . .?"

"Why don't you see if . . .?"

5. *The Screened Question* is afraid to express an open desire. The questioner asks with a hidden motive, hoping the other will suggest what he or she wants to have happen.

"What would you like to do . . .?"

6. *The Trap Question* attempts to trap the person into a vulnerable position which will prove him wrong with his own words.

"Is it true that you once . . .?"

REAL QUESTIONS
—Probe for facts
—Seek information
—Ask for observations of feelings, values, inferences

NOT REAL QUESTIONS
—Limit information
—Make demands
—Seek to control actions

—Conceal feelings and values
—Infer improper motives

Which of the following are real questions and which are not real? Mark R for real, N for not real.

_____ a. What time is it?
_____ b. Where do you buy your shoes?
_____ c. Where do you think you're going?
_____ d. Are you ever going to clean up your room?
_____ e. Who told you you could use the car?
_____ f. Who are you meeting for lunch?
_____ g. Don't you believe you should wait?
_____ h. Since you're a woman, wouldn't you vote for birth control?

Statement (a) is likely a real question unless it's a father asking his daughter's date. In such a case he probably knows it's after midnight and Dad is really saying "go home." Statement (b) is also a real question asking for information—unless it's a catty remark which says, (1) "Those shoes are awful; do you always shop at the Goodwill Store?" or (2) "Say! I wish I could afford expensive shoes like those."

Generally speaking (a), (b), and (f) are the only real questions. And again generally speaking (c), (d), (e), (g), and (h) are not real questions but are traps (c, e) or commands (d), hypothetical or screen (h), and leading (g).

Which of the following are characteristics of real and not real questions? Mark R for real, N for not real.

_____ a. Make demands
_____ b. Seek information
_____ c. Infer improper motives
_____ d. Seek to control actions
_____ e. Probe for facts
_____ f. Ask for observations of feelings

Real questions seek information, probe for facts, ask for observations of feelings, values, or inferences. Thus if you marked R for (b), (e), and (f) you are correct. Questions that are not real make demands (a), infer improper motives (c), and seek to control actions (d). They also limit information and conceal feelings and values.

Skill 3: Select specific words and statements the other can understand.

As you project your intended message, use specific words and statements. Select your words with care, not only to explain clearly but to meet the other person's ability to interpret. We live in a world of many languages in one. A dentist and a farmer have a number of words in common which they both will easily understand. But let them begin to speak in terms of their own vocational skill and misunderstanding may result.

Skill 4: Speak with respect for your listener.

In a conflict, feelings are very much involved. We will explore this special area more thoroughly in a later chapter. The main idea is to be open and honest about your feelings. And be considerate of the other's feelings.

If you want to resolve the conflicts you have in your family or with friends you will need to accept a few rules. Even if it's one-sided and you are the only one fighting by the rules, stick with them.

1. No shouting or name calling. And above all, no blows. Leave the fisticuffs to the professional boxers. Avoid judgments and accusations like—

"You're always late."

"You never listen."

"You're a stupid fool."

"You like being nasty, don't you?"

2. Keep it present, here and now. Don't drag up all the bad past history and throw it at the other person. Things that disturb you in a relationship should be talked about as they happen, instead of being stored up in a pile of hurt feelings and irritations, and then dumped on the other person all at once.

3. Don't pull in rumors or gossip. Deal with what you know, not in speculations.

4. Do not force the other to change. Avoid pushy statements or questions. Even though the conflict may heat up, allow the other the privilege to use the experience as he sees fit, in his own time. "Treat others as you would like them to treat you. . . . Be compassionate as your Father is compassionate" (Luke 6:31, 36, NEB).

John Wallen, in his studies on communications, says the attitude should not be, "Who's right and who's wrong," but rather, "What can each of us learn from this that will improve our relationship?"

In working toward resolving conflict it is necessary to consider the feelings and perceiving style of your listener. True or false?

In shaping your comments and statements to get through to the other, you will need to take into consideration the perceiving style and the emotional state of your listener. The statement is true.

In speaking with respect for the other you will do certain things and avoid others. Select from the following those which represent a helpful approach (Mark *Yes*) and those to be avoided (mark *No*).

_____ a. When she argues about what I did this morning, I'll remind her how she goofed last week.

_____ b. If he swears at me again, I'm going to swear right back.

———— c. I'll try to work it so she won't feel like she has to change just to suit me.

———— d. He's got some explaining to do since Alice told me she's heard he's playing around.

The problem with dragging up her failure last week is (1) you are making today's situation muddy and (2) you'll build the conflict instead of reduce it. Thus (a) is No. So is (b) for similar reasons. Try breaking the pattern of hurt—hurt back. Statement (d) is No also. Check out the rumors before you believe them. Remember gossip stands as good a chance of being wrong as right.

The only Yes here is (c). If in your conflict you don't try to coerce one another, you may surprise each other by the better attitudes both of you develop.

Skill 5: Check your message with the listener.

In a conflict you can't afford to be misunderstood. If your statement is important check with the other person, even if you have to repeat yourself.

"Does what I just said make sense to you? Did you understand that I meant. . . ?"

Remember how difficult it is for you to understand and express your own feelings and ideas—and how much more difficult it must be for someone else to grasp clearly what you mean. Particularly during a conflict there is the increased likelihood of misunderstanding when the person listening to you is in a heightened emotional state and defending his or her point of view.

Patience is a gold-plated virtue in times of conflict. Patience and gentleness and kindness are qualities of spirit you don't feel much like expressing in a contentious situation. Unless you are unusually gifted with an accepting nature, you'd just as soon wring the other person's neck at times.

It is at this point the reality of the power of God to help can come home to you—when you least feel like remaining calm and patient and helpful to the other person. Yet if at that moment—by faith in the spirit of Christ to help—you deliberately choose to put away rage and harsh thoughts toward the other person, you can begin to experience what the Apostle Paul wrote about to the Christians at Colossae:

"As, therefore, God's picked representatives of the new humanity, purified and beloved of God himself, be merciful in action, kindly in heart, humble in mind. Accept life, and be most patient and tolerant with one another, always ready to forgive if you have a difference with anyone. Forgive as freely as the Lord has forgiven you. And, above everything else, be truly loving, for love is the golden chain of all the virtues. Let the peace of Christ rule in your hearts . . ." (Colossians 3:12-15, Phillips).

12
The Art of Listening

Darlene and Bill were "mutually incompatible." Or so they thought. Because of a common "escape plan" they both shared, they both anticipated divorce in their situation. As Bill put it, "We should never have married in the first place, so divorce really is the only sensible thing for us to consider."

Then a friend told them their problem wasn't incompatible personalities but poor communication.

"Neither one of us was a good listener," Darlene reports. "We were both working and busy and we had a lot of friends. From the time we were married we drifted apart."

Before they were married Darlene and Bill spent a lot of time together and enjoyed one another. Bill has only come to accept that memory recently. He had convinced himself they never really had anything going for them.

"I got so I didn't even want to try to talk with Darlene," he explains. "She was assertive, and obviously not listening, and—"

"And I was always interrupting him," Darlene interjected, "because I wanted him to hear me. But he never had time. If I didn't get it said, pretty soon he'd look at his watch and run for the door."

Bill smiled to soften what he was about to say. "I feel you're still uncertain whether I'll listen to you. I developed some habits I'm not proud of now. But I'm learning. And it's going to take practice."

"And I've got to learn to be patient," Darlene added. Their decision to give their marriage a second chance was also mutually arrived at, shortly after an evening with their friend who encouraged them to try a "listening session." After a rough, wrangling first hour the friend succeeded in getting them to hear and feel and respect the other's point of view. They're lucky to have made the discovery in only one session.

"We talked half the night—the first time really in over four years," Bill explained.

Listening or perceiving accurately is by far the most difficult part of a conversation. Add the tensions and emotions of a conflict and the difficulty in perceiving (or listening) is multiplied many times over.

If our style of handling conflict is to YIELD, we are likely to be overly sensitive to any hostility in a conversation that might be a hazard to our relationships. And we may fake agreement and interest we don't feel just to affirm how congenial we still are.

If we use a WIN style, we may infer from the words that the speaker needs correcting and our responses may begin frequently with "No," or "But." And if our convictions are being challenged we may simply hear what we want to hear and close out all the rest.

If you work with a COMPROMISE style, you may perceive in a speaker's words opportunities for negotiation—even ones that aren't there. It is possible to pick out facts and points to organize a compromise while missing the meanings and their import for your relationships.

A WITHDRAW person often "reads" threats into what is being said. And then listening becomes an operation in covert criticism, judging the other person's intended message by his appearance or delivery—how he says it and not what he is saying.

Consequently, to become more expert in RESOLVING conflict, all of us need to improve our perceiving or listening skills.

David Augsburger in his book, *The Love-Fight*, describes perceiving as "hearing what another says, how it is said, and what feeling is conveyed. To hear with an inner ear is to tune in to the feelings, the hurts, the angers, the demands of another.

"I want to hear you, and not hear myself interpreting you. I am aware of two strong tendencies: (1) to 'read in' things I feel as I listen, and miss what you are wanting to tell me; and (2) to 'read out' and totally miss what I don't want to hear from you because it threatens, confronts, rejects, or ignores me and my viewpoint.

"I want to hear you accurately, so I'll need to check out what I hear at crucial points to be as sure as I can that my meanings match your meanings. I get an inkling of what your meanings are from your words, your tone of voice, your face, gestures, and body movements. But it is only an inkling. I must check it out at times by replaying what I heard for your approval, until you agree that you have been heard."

Perceiving is an adjustment of my understanding of

your words, gestures, and emotions to the meaning you intend the words, gestures, and emotions to convey.

Remember, meaning is *not* in words you speak, or the expression on your face, or the excitement in your voice. What you mean by what you project lies back of all of these in your mind and personality.

In this chapter we will consider six skills by which we can improve our listening and perceiving:

1. Concentrate on the present.
2. Defuse the message.
3. Slow your evaluation.
4. Sift the irrelevant.
5. Check the message.
6. Register acceptance and empathy.

Skill 1: Concentrate on the present.

In a conflict, particularly if the person is close to you—spouse, parent, child, sister, brother, partner, work mate—it is difficult to listen to the *present*. You are apt to remember another conflict with the person and another hurt, and use that as a filter to hear what the other is saying today.

As you listen concentrate on *present* statements, on what the person is saying *now*. Even if the person brings up past problems, look for the *present reason*. Look at him or her. Try to close out distractions. By observing closely, attempt to connect the words and gestures as you reach for present meanings.

Skill 2: Defuse the message.

Some words are triggers for you ("whitey," "pig," "communist," "four-letter words," as well as words with intense private and personal meaning). When you hear them, you are likely to respond emotionally to your meanings and miss the other's intent.

Learn to recognize your own trigger words and defuse them. Try to understand why you have reacted to them in the past. Acknowledge to yourself that some people will have other meanings. Expand your meanings to include those of others so you are better equipped to understand *their* message.

Skill 3: Slow your evaluation.

Too often we have our minds made up about what the speaker has said before he says it—particularly if we don't agree with what we think he's going to say.

Wait. Hear the other person through before you evaluate the message. Deliberately allow the other the privilege of a differing point of view. Attempt to understand the other's perspectives behind the words or gestures while you are hearing them.

Try to clear your own expectations. If you expect the other person to be hostile, you will see "hostility" where it doesn't exist. Do not prejudge the emotional level of the other's statements.

Remember, whatever the other person is saying can be a starting point for an improved relationship between you. But this starts by understanding as much as you can—as sympathetically as you can.

Skill 4: Sift the irrelevant.

Few of us speak simply. We add details, go on long detours, overemphasize to make a point. A conflict situation encourages elaborations, making it more difficult to hear what is really being said.

In hearing the other person completely, try to sift out the detours that are truly irrelevant. His phone may ring and he might explode in exasperation at the interruption—be careful that you do not carry over the explosion into the conversation. If you do you might misjudge exasperation for anger.

But take care not to sift out something that may seem an irrelevant detour to you which is to the other person an illustration of his point.

You are angry with someone who is supposed to be your best friend. She seems to have misunderstood your intentions about your plans for the next few weeks and accuses you of lying to her. You want to clear up the misunderstanding quickly but she doesn't want to listen because she seems to have more to say to you. Check which one or more might be appropriate courses of action.

_____ a. Tell her to shut up and listen.
_____ b. Insist she concentrate on what you are
　　　　 trying to explain.
_____ c. Sift the irrelevant comments she makes and
　　　　 try and find the real hurt behind her anger.
_____ d. Concentrate your attention on her message.
_____ e. Slow your evaluation.

Action (a) is apt to heat up the conflict and get you nowhere. (b) is not likely to help either because she isn't at the point of listening. She seems to be communicating a hurt (c) she wants you to feel and understand, so you better concentrate your attention on her message (d). And that means sifting her message for the relevant comments too. And slow up on trying to answer her anger until you are sure you understand why she feels that way (e). So (c), (d), and (e) are the most appropriate actions for you to take.

Skill 5: Check the message.

You don't need to be in doubt about the other's meaning. Check your perceptions with him and find out.

You may say, "I think this is what you mean. Am I right?" and then feed back your understanding of his message. If you are alert to the feelings he is expressing—in gestures, tone of voice, facial expression—you can add these elements together and check out the other's *feelings* too.

John Wallen gives the example: " 'I get the impression you are angry with me. Are you?'

"(NOT: 'Why are you so angry with me?' That is mind reading not perception checking.)

"Note that a perception check *describes* the other's feelings, and *does not express disapproval or approval.* It merely conveys, 'This is how I understand your feelings. Am I accurate?' "

Skill 6: Register acceptance and empathy.

When you have checked your perception with the other person, do more than just let him know you understand what he's saying.

Tell him you see what he's getting at. Do it gently. And mean it. Show by your acceptance that while you may not agree with what he is saying you respect him as a person.

Many times a conflict heats up because one person feels he hasn't been understood and, even worse, that he is being rejected for his views. Frequently when a person believes his views are understood—and accepted as a point of view—tensions are relieved.

Accepting a person's integrity to hold a viewpoint does not mean agreeing with it. In fact, your own differing opinion may show up most clearly when the other person sees that you understand and acknowlege his opinion. In other words, it may be that you will influence the other person most with your differing point of view when he realizes you understand his.

But don't just try this as a way to get him to change! People change when they want to, when they feel it is necessary for their own purposes, not before. An old saying expresses it well, "You can't push string." Be understanding, not coercive or judgmental. You can hang onto your own convictions and still be understanding.

Empathize. Try to feel as the other feels. This may be particularly difficult to do when you have feelings of your own you wish he or she might acknowledge. Yet try to feel the hurt he or she is projecting. Your empathy, your reaching out, will communicate itself and help the other person to express feelings more clearly.

Remember that best friend who was angry with you in the last question? After listening to her, you discover she expected you to tell her when you were going to plan a change in your work schedule. Then she accuses you again of lying to her. Check which of the following might be most helpful in resolving the conflict.

_____ a. Explain you didn't realize your work schedule was any of her business.

_____ b. Tell her you don't like being called a liar.

_____ c. Before you evaluate her message, remind yourself not to become distracted by your hostile reaction to "liar" or "lying."

_____ d. Check back with her on what she might mean.

Telling someone in anger to "get lost" or "mind your own business" (a) seems to give a lot of us a perverse sort of pleasure, but if we are to resolve our conflicts satisfactorily, this isn't going to be very helpful. Nor is it quite safe to use answer (b) until we have learned the skills (in Part IV) on how to express our feelings clearly in a way that encourages reconciliation. So neither (a) nor (b) are appropriate at this point.

You will find it useful, as in (c), to defuse words that the other person uses in hostility. It will allow you to hear and grasp her meaning and leave you reasonably free—even in your anger—to work toward reconciliation.

And (d) will be helpful also. To clarify matters you might ask her something like, "You feel that when I told you I'd let you know what I was going to do that it included letting you in on planning a work schedule?" She might answer, "No, I don't expect to plan your schedule for you. But I do have some suggestions to offer." It is always useful to check out the message you are interpreting to make sure you understand the other's point of view.

13
Analyze Your Progress

In Part II we have explored some basic concepts of communication and a number of skills to improve your abilities to perceive meanings in what someone says to you. Also we have tried out some skills in single-level projecting. If you wish to check out what you have learned, here are seven overview questions.

Check one. Which is faster?
_____ a. Thinking speed
_____ b. Speaking speed?

If you missed (a) you may want to recheck chapter 8.

Which of the following is most difficult to communicate?
_____ a. Event or process
_____ b. Concept, opinion, or emotion
_____ c. Fact

Facts are easier to explain than events or processes. Most of us find it hardest of all to explain our feelings, opinions, and ideas, thus answer (b) is correct [from Chapter 8].

Select from the following to fill in the sentence:
                    words   people
Meaning is found in (a)_____ not in (b)_____.

Although we tend to expect meaning to be in the words people use, the full or actual meaning remains with the people who express the words. The appropriate answer is (a) people, (b) words [from Chapter 9].

Which (one or more) of the following are important for you to use in sending a clear message to another person?

_____ a. Attention
_____ b. Words
_____ c. Distractions
_____ d. Drives
_____ e. Gestures

In a message, words, drives, and gestures are important parts. Attention is usually thought of as a listening skill, and distractions work against a clear message [from Chapter 10].

Certain trigger words have extraordinarily strong meaning for you. When you hear them in a conversation, you are likely to:

_____ a. Believe the speaker means the same as you do.
_____ b. Be distracted from the speaker's message.

Words like "communist," "chauvinist," "red-neck" are examples of trigger words. All of us have a number of these kinds of words which are apt to excite us and perhaps distract us from the speaker's message. Also, we are likely to believe the speaker has the same meaning and may thus interpret this message incorrectly. Both answers are correct. [from Chapter 10].

Helpful speaking or projecting skills involve which (one or more) of the following?

_____ a. Being honest
_____ b. Not revealing your feelings
_____ c. Saying you know more than you do
_____ d. Using questions that are real
_____ e. Not using pressures on the other to change

You can hardly communicate properly without revealing

your feelings, so (b) is incorrect. And so is (c), although many of us try to win an argument by claiming we know more than we do. Answers (a), (d), and (e) are correct and are skills you will want to develop [Chapter 11].

Helpful perceiving skills include which (one or more) of the following:

_____ a. Testing your interpretation with the speaker
_____ b. Paying attention only to the meanings you understand
_____ c. Not jumping to conclusions
_____ d. Telling the speaker to cool down if he gets excited

In many situations telling the speaker to cool down is apt to increase the excitement, so (d) isn't very helpful. And (b) is also a mistake, if you only give attention to the parts of a message you think you understand. In this question (a) and (c) are the important perceiving skills. Others include sifting out the detours and distractions, concentrating on the present, checking out the message with the person, and showing that you understand and feel with him [Chapter 12].

Meaning is a meeting of minds. And minds which meet are on their way to mutual understanding.

Frequently a person says one thing but means a great deal more. One day, as Jesus and His disciples walked along, they saw a man who had been blind from birth.

"Rabbi," the disciples asked, "whose sin caused this man's blindness, his own or his parents?"

You can almost hear Jesus asking Himself what the real question was that they were asking, perhaps something like, "If God really loves us, why does He allow suffering? Because if it's caused by sin, then what about this man—and others like him?"

Jesus *listened.* He perceived the thought behind the words. And in the sweep of events that followed, He gave His followers a crash course in human nature. There are some interesting insights into communication skills too. It is well worth reading this account in John 9.

Jesus answered that it wasn't a matter of sin. He explained that the man's blindness—like any human problem, physical, emotional, or relational—is an opportunity for us to see the faith of man and the power of God at work in developing a true humanity.

In this situation Jesus knew that a wordy reponse (to what was basically a philosophical question) would not be enough. Instead He demonstrated the underlying realities in the terribly human situation. And so He healed the blind man's eyes in a way that Jesus' identity remained unknown to him.

> Jesus uses a demonstration here to convey His meaning. In the Sermon on the mount He used words to convey His meaning. According to our description of projecting or sending a message, He selected His words and demonstration from which of the following?
>> _____ a. Perceiving method
>> _____ b. Sending equipment
>> _____ c. Distractions

The selection Jesus decided to use in communicating the power of God came from (b), His sending equipment.

The situation then began to develop in widening shock waves. The former blind man's neighbors were full of questions. How was he healed? Who healed him? The man's answers were as truthful as he could make them—but not very satisfying. So they took him to the Pharisees.

The Pharisees were prejudiced against Jesus, particularly since He had healed the man on the Sabbath when no one should work. They debated among themselves. "The man who did this," one side questioned, "cannot be from God because He does not obey the Sabbath law." But others demanded, "How could a man who is a sinner do such wonderful works as these?"

From your understanding of our study, which (one or more) of the following correctly describes the first side's question?

____ a. Real
____ b. Hypothetical (used to criticize)
____ c. Not real
____ d. Command (demands action)
____ e. Trap question

The first question in the debate doesn't ask for facts or observations as a real question would, but infers that "something is wrong" in a way that seems to criticize Jesus for healing on the Sabbath and the blind man for being healed, so the correct answers are (c) Not real, and (b) Hypothetical. And in the sense that there is an implied threat to both Jesus and the blind man it can also be considered a trap too (e).

So the Pharisees centered their debate on the blind man: "What do you say about him?" Now, obviously the once-blind man would be riding high and pretty much in favor of whoever it was who had healed him. So again, he projected from his deepest feelings. "He is a prophet," he answered.

But the Jews were unwilling to accept the factual report of the man. They asked his parents to verify their son's story that he had indeed been born blind. But the anger and threat came through the Pharisees' projecting system clearly. Clearly enough that the man's parents feared for their future in the community.

So when they were asked to explain how their blind son could now see, they ducked the question. "He's old enough to speak for himself. Ask him!"

The parent's statement is (check one):
_____ a. A clear, specific, single-level expression which explains their point of view.
_____ b. A two-level expression which hides their point of view.

Because of their fear, the parents avoid an open statement of opinion; so you will have checked (b).

This time, the once-blind man threw the deceit of the Pharisees questions back at them. The Pharisees wanted to pin blame on someone—hopefully Jesus—in order to reject the obvious: a direct, visible, popular communication of life-changing concern from God to humankind. So the man retorted, "I've told you before. Weren't you listening? Why do you want to hear it again? Are you wanting to be His disciples too?"

Which of the following identify the once-blind man's questions?
_____ a. Probe for facts (real questions)
_____ b. Infer improper motives (not-real questions)

It is clear that the man is upset at the two-level, two-faced attitude of the Pharisees, so he lashes out with these questions which really don't call for a factual response (a) but infer improper motives (b), so they are not-real questions.

Then the result Jesus expected, and wanted others to notice, happened. The Pharisees turned on the blind man in fury. "We are Moses' disciples. We know that God spoke to Moses; as for that fellow, we do not even know where he comes from!"

The man answered: "How strange! You don't know where He comes from, but He opened my eyes! . . . Since the beginning of the world it has never been heard of that Someone opened the eyes of a blind man; unless this Man came from God, He would not be able to do a thing."

They answered back, "You were born and raised in sin—and you are trying to teach us?" And they threw him out of the meetinghouse.

In spite of the realities of the situation, the Pharisees could not accept them and preferred the unreal world of their own making. It was the same kind of double-think which later drove the religious leaders to crucify Jesus. Although His notable words and actions combined to identify Him as God-with-us, the religious leaders measured Him against their preconceptions—and like the saying, "My mind is made up, don't confuse me with facts," they chose misconceptions over reality.

So what else is new? We're still doing much the same thing today.

Part III
A Larger Love

14
The Different Kinds of Love

Love, as strong as Death, retrieves as well.
—*Elizabeth Barrett Browning*

Love is patient and kind; love is not jealous, or conceited, or proud; love is not ill-mannered, or selfish, or irritable; love does not keep a record of wrongs; love is not happy with evil, but is happy with the truth. Love never gives up: its faith, hope, and patience never fail. 1 Corinthians 13:4-7, TEV.

Whatever our conflicts may be, there is the hope of love—not sentimental and syrupy cliché's, but tough-minded, responsible, forgiven-and-forgiving love—to reach across our differences toward reconciliation.

Love is a many-splendored thing. Friendship. Affection. Falling-in-love love. Child-parent, parent-child devotion. Glorious day, glad-I'm-alive love of everything. Down-in-the-dumps but thank-God-anyway love of living.

Love is the glue of life. By love we belong in the family; in the kinship of humanity and the fellowship of God. Even when we are feeling most unloved and unlovable, we are targets of the power of love. *For God is love and we are who He loves.*

The Bible stresses one major theme throughout—how men and women, caught up in the tensions of living and short on time, temper, and tranquillity, may be transformed by love into people of love. And with its power we in turn become able to move mountains of hostility, to fill canyons of distrust and despair, to smooth the rough places of broken promises and dreams, and prepare a highway for reconciliation.

But love is a discovered ability. We have only been given samples to start from. Most of us know just enough about the various powers of love to get ourselves into trouble, and not nearly enough to work our way through to the land we promised ourselves on the other side.

In Part III we will look at the various intensities of love. You will have the opportunity to compare your present understandings of love to several views, traditional and modern. Hopefully, you will be able to adapt your concepts to include several new and useful understandings.

Additionally you will test yourself against a group of forgiving-trusting and compassion-caring behaviors.

Next comes an exploration of the skills you can learn in order to love responsibly when it is difficult for you to do so.

Finally, the skills of trusting, caring, and responsible love are studied in the context of marriage, where so many conflicts and misunderstandings are excited by the presence—or absence—of sex drives.

"I think I love him. When I'm not hating him so much.

"I mean—he just expects me to take him as he is. But

he wants me to change into some ideal playmate, to like all the things he likes.

"If I want us to do something together, he might like it. Or he might yawn his way through it like a bored brat.

"Yet . . . I guess I love him. And I think he loves me.

"If he just weren't so insufferably self-right all the time!"

Love to most of us has its major drive in feelings. When we love another person we feel love in varying intensities. There are sexual overtones and undercurrents—even in parent-child relationships—intermixed with feelings of friendship and companionship.

And if pushed to the extremes of need, other qualities rise up, best thought of as self-giving, even self-sacrificing love, extending beyond family and friend to neighbor and even stranger.

    Love is—
        _____ a. Something that happens to you
        _____ b. Something you choose to do
        _____ c. A discovered ability

It wouldn't be quite fair to eliminate any of the answers as being incorrect, but (b) and (c) are much more to the point of real love than the glandular emotion which we often call love in (a).

In his book, *The Four Loves*, C. S. Lewis reaches back to Hebrew, Christian, and Greek concepts to identify four qualities of love—*affection, friendship, eros,* and *charity*. He groups these in two kinds, Need-love and Gift-love: love that we seek out to satisfy our needs and love that we give of ourselves to meet the needs of others.

In his interpretation of the four loves, the first quality,

affection—while it can exist by itself—colors the other loves and provides an atmosphere in which friendship and eros may grow.

In our modern world we do not see much of the second love Lewis describes, *friendship*. We have its beginnings in companionship, but true friendship moves beyond to share mutual interests and insights and goals. In *eros*, lovers are face to face with eyes fixed on each other. By contrast, in *friendship*, the friends are side by side with eyes ahead on common interests.

Eros is "being in love," the love which leads to sexual desire and marriage. Unless subject to higher principles, it can become an evil rather than a good.

Lewis's final love, *charity*, rises above all the earthly loves. As we love others selflessly, we are beginning to experience the quality of love God has for us.

It may seem confusing to divide "love" into such pieces, but all of us can distinguish between "like" and "love," even though we may not be able to describe the difference adequately. Yet if we are to become more skilled in resolving our conflicts, we need to become more aware of our feelings and why they move us as they do. That's why an exploration of the kinds or qualities of love is worthwhile.

> Exploring the different qualities of love has value to us because (check the appropriate statement)—
> _____ a. We use differing loves with different people
> _____ b. We can understand our feelings and be better prepared to deal with them
> _____ c. Both of the above

When it comes to a situation of conflict, we need to understand our feelings and the possibility of going beyond the hurts and tensions of conflict with self-giving love to enable us to work toward healthy solutions. And it also makes common sense to assume that we use the different kinds of qualities of love with different people, so both of the statements are appropriate. Thus if you checked (c) you are correct.

Let's explore one other way of dividing up this thing called love. We won't look at it as only an emotion or an expression of glandular drives or the exercise of will-power but all of these in combination, *in the development of a mature personality or self.*

We can see it in three parts or aspects. First is *self-love,* an inward, absorbing love that seeks to fulfill our personal needs and drives. It trusts loving parents and friends—and a loving God—to help meet our basic wants. Uncontrolled, it becomes selfish and works to destroy our relationships.

Some will ask, "Isn't self-love always selfish?" Not at all. Without respect for yourself and a prudent concern for your physical and emotional needs, you're not likely to develop into a person with love to share with others.

Jesus had a healthy self-love. And He reaffirms the biblical command to "love thy neighbor *as thyself.*" The love Jesus lived out was big enough to include Himself and others.

Some people can't stand themselves. Nothing they do is right to themselves. Frequently this attitude spills over to envelop others as well. The inability to love others begins for them in a lack of self-respecting love for themselves.

And as far as selfishness goes, in the view of psychoanalyst Erich Fromm, the selfish person doesn't love himself too much, but too little.

Which (one or more) of the following statements is appropriate regarding self-love?

_____ a. I can love myself as long as I love others more.

_____ b. If I love myself a lot I can love others a lot.

_____ c. If I love properly, I love everybody—God, neighbor, and myself.

Statement (a) seems to indicate a measuring out of love, "so much for neighbor, so much for me," and inaccurately describes the nature of love. Choice (b) seems to be closer, at least in its enthusiastic abundance. But (c) is a more appropriate statement about self-love, in that if we love properly we love all, including and equally ourselves.

A second level of love is *self-sharing*, growing out of and beyond the first. We see it in the joy of friendships and in the companionship and mutual sexual satisfaction many married couples experience. Self-sharing makes possible a healthy meeting of another's needs while achieving a reasonable satisfaction of one's own.

In sharing we can see that love is larger than ourselves. And that it isn't meant to be as directional or exclusive as we may have thought. Love is a quality of being, an expression of who we are and how we act toward life, toward "neighbor as well as self."

The third and completing aspect of love is *self-giving*, going beyond the need to satisfy personal wants to give of ourselves to others, often in spite of personal discomfort.

Many of us are reasonably capable of self-love. Many of us have matured enough to be able to share ourselves easily with friends and neighbors, and intimately with a spouse. Yet very few of us dare to grow to the level of self-giving love which, as Jesus exemplified, is able knowingly to lay down its life for others if need be.

Complete the sentence with the appropriate statement. Self-giving love—

_____ a. Seeks the mutual achievement of needs.

_____ b. Attempts to go beyond personal goals to meet the need of another.

_____ c. Tries to satisfy personal needs.

Self-giving love goes a second mile beyond personal satisfactions to meet the needs of another person, thus (b) is the appropriate answer. This is a mature expression of love which is not meant to spoil the other person. Simply giving in to the immature demands of another can be selfish. To give an alcoholic friend your last five dollars for the drink he demands is not as self-giving as risking his anger by saying no and explaining why.

Love involves which (one or more) of the following characteristics?

_____ a. Erotic attraction

_____ b. Selfishness

_____ c. Neighbor-love

_____ d. Charity

If you checked all but (b), you are correct. While self-love is a characteristic of love, selfishness is not.

Another way of looking at love is to see its intensities across a spectrum of those to whom we give our love. We can see a logical variation in our feelings toward those we barely know across to those we know most intimately.

We reserve certain actions for the intimacy of marriage. Certain expressions of concern and love we keep for our children and closest friends which we would not include in relationships with acquaintances or those we barely know.

Also, while we could feel a liking or *affection* toward

our work mates or a neighbor or even an acquaintance, that feeling is not likely to be as warm as our affection toward a close friend or the deep affections we hold for our children or spouse.

A parallel progression of feeling we will recognize in the categories of *friendship* and *intimate love*—unless those relationships become strained or broken.

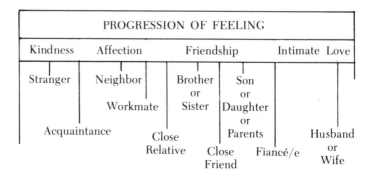

PROGRESSION OF FEELING					
Kindness	Affection		Friendship		Intimate Love
Stranger	Neighbor		Brother or Sister	Son or Daughter or Parents	
	Workmate				
Acquaintance		Close Relative			Husband or Wife
			Close Friend	Fiancé/e	

Nevertheless, cutting across all of these intensities, the quality of self-giving love covers and colors the whole range of relationships from the stranger to the lover. It influences the meaning of affection and friendship and intimate love. Let's take a closer look at self-giving love.

15
The Strength of Self-Giving Love

We can twist affection, friendship, and intimacy until they are no longer love. It is a very short path from affection to antipathy, from friendship to frustration, from intimacy to indignation.

And here is where the godlike quality of self-giving love can work its miracles. But what is a "godlike" quality of love? At the risk of oversimplifying, the purpose of the Bible has always been to document some of the acts of God toward humanity to show that self-giving love is the chief characteristic of God *and of the life He designed for us to live.* The Hebrews who thought through the "meaning" of Jesus' life and His teachings came to this conclusion—but only after His resurrection from death.

Before His resurrection, Jesus' message from God to humanity didn't seem to get through. Jesus was misunderstood, although His actions and words were aimed at revealing the true character of God in contrast to the many misconceptions and man-made creations given the name "God."

Even His closest followers failed to grasp what Jesus showed by His life—that God is love, self-giving love. In one situation shortly before His crucifixion (recorded in John 14) Jesus was explaining that His time to return to His Father had come, but that He would soon come back to lead them to their own fulfillment. Therefore they should not be troubled by the immediate events but simply trust Him as they would trust God.

At that point He was interrupted. He went on later to complete what He was about to say, telling them that when He goes away God will send His Spirit to them in His place. But before He was able to finish, He was sidetracked by the disciples' confusion.

Thomas wanted to know where it was that He was going. Jesus' reply to him focused on God, His Father, and that the disciples should know who and where the Father was because they had known Jesus.

Philip, one of the disciples, seemed to speak for them all at that point. He simply doesn't understand. Who really is this Father Jesus says they should know about? Jesus replied, "Have I been with you so long, and yet you do not know me, Philip? He who has seen me has seen the Father; how can you say, 'Show us the Father'? Do you not believe that I am in the Father and the Father in me? The words that I say to you I do not speak on my own authority; but the Father who dwells in me does his works. Believe me that I am in the Father and the Father in me; or else believe me for the sake of the works themselves" (John 14:9-11, RSV).

Philip is like the rest of us. We expect God to be a dozen other things than the kind of self-giving love that Jesus showed by His life and death. He demonstrated the love of God in giving new life to many of the castoffs of society, in one instance forgiving a prostitute and freeing her from the prison of her own making. These acts of

God-love offended the religious leaders, and Jesus criticized them for caring more for their interpretations of the commandments than for the people.

Yet the people misunderstood His message, just as the disciples did. They cheered Him into Jerusalem, expecting the Savior King to sweep away the armies of the Roman Empire. Instead Jesus drove the tradesmen out of the temple and said His kingdom was not of this world. And this King of kings took a towel and a basin of water and washed His disciples' feet!

Humility in an almighty Lord? How could Jesus stoop to wash the feet of His followers? Perhaps this demonstration of self-giving love is one of Jesus' strongest yet most misunderstood messages to our world today. As He told His disciples, "Do you realize what I have just done to you? You call me 'Teacher' and 'Lord' and you are quite right, for I am your teacher and your Lord. But if I, your teacher and Lord, have washed your feet, you must be ready to wash one another's feet. I have given you this as an example so that you may do as I have done" (John 13:13-15, Phillips).

God-love represents (check one or more)—
_____ a. The kind of love God has for humanity
_____ b. A feeling of love that only the very religious person can have for God
_____ c. A quality of love we can extend to others by faith

Many people prefer to think that only the very religious can love God. This makes it convenient to avoid the challenges of Jesus to live out the love that God can work through us by faith—the same kind of love God has for humanity. Thus (b) is incorrect while (a) and (c) are correct.

If Jesus revealed the character of God, which one or more

of the following are appropriate comments about that character as we studied it?

_____ a. God is interested only in those who love Him.
_____ b. His love is self-giving.
_____ c. His kind of love is the major characteristic our lives are designed to express.

The remarkable message of Jesus is that God loves the "sinner." As He said, "I have come to seek and to save those who are lost." So (a) is not one you should have checked. Both (b) and (c) are appropriate comments about God-love. It's difficult to accept the idea that humankind, with all our inhumanity to fellowmen, is designed to love with God-love. Yet the possibility can become a reality in us as we begin to live in the way God intended for us.

We are not used to the idea of humility. Or self-giving love. Generally this amounts to weakness in the common view. Occasionally a television drama will show a policeman giving his life to save a buddy, and it can be a pretty moving experience to watch such an epic, if it isn't superficial in its treatment.

On rarer occasions a drama brings us a man who gives his life for a whole neighborhood, even a community which has been hostile to him and misunderstanding. In such a story we are getting closer to the message of God-love in Jesus Christ. "The proof of God's amazing love is this: that it was *while we were sinners* that Christ died for us" (Romans 5:8, Phillips).

We deeply appreciate that kind of heroic act. *But we would rather not volunteer for such a mission ourselves.*

Yet that is precisely the case here. Not that all of us will be asked to face execution in place of another or leap in front of a truck to save a stranger's life. But the quality of the love that is prepared to act in such a way is asked of every one of us.

This quality of love cares for the hurts of others even in conflict. It is the love that says, "For me, the other person's worth and growth are as important as my own."

We will explore some skills that go into self-giving love later. It is important here to know that we will need more than skills in order to actually give such love—particularly during a conflict when we are much more likely to become self-serving than self-giving.

And so we will need help. We will need resources and strengths beyond any we have experienced before. Again the message of Jesus is that help is available—all the help we need. The idea of Christianity is that if we are willing to *love totally*—to love God as well as ourselves as well as our neighbor as well as our enemy—then God will enable us to do so.

We simply choose to love. It is an act of will as well as of faith. Faith in itself is an act of will which says, "Whether I believe or can logically accept that you are there, God, and can help me to become love like this, nevertheless I believe and accept it and act upon it—Lord, help my unbelief!"

Match each of the statements below to one of the characteristics of love listed:

1. Self-giving love
2. Selfishness
3. Self-love

_____ a. To think first of yourself and your needs so that you can look after somebody else when the need arises

_____ b. To adjust your attitudes toward others so that you are as concerned for their worth and growth as for your own

_____ c. To have a character of love which includes yourself as much as others

*Item (b) is self-giving love, 1. Choice (c) is one of the
aspects of self-love, 3. Now what about (a)? If the purpose
of (a) is genuine in practice as well as intention, then we can
say that this statement shows some aspects of self-love, even
self-giving love. Yet (a) is also the kind of deception we
often practice on ourselves when we are really being selfish.
We cover it up with statements like, "I will make a lot of
money so I can give some to the poor."*

Self-giving love is strong because it can draw upon the
limitless resources of God. God is self-giving love, and
He is able to develop in us the similar characteristic
through the actions of self-giving faith.

16
Skills of Self-Giving Love

A. Forgiveness: Respects and Trusts

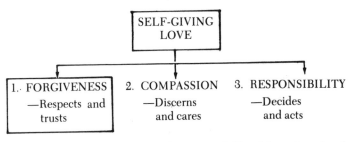

Now let's look at the self-giving skills of love involved in three areas: (1) forgiveness, (2) compassion, and (3) responsibility. In this chapter we'll focus on forgiveness.

Should we "forgive" someone for being different? To get from where we are in our thinking about someone else, we may have to do this. Prejudice is a peculiar passion. It has no basis in fact, only in fear. We fear what we do not know. If another person is different from us, we have difficulty in knowing or understanding the messages we receive from him.

If the person is of a different background, another race, speaks another language, has differing social and political and religious views we are likely to be insecure in any relationships with him. And we will likely miss by wide margins any judgments we make on his attitudes and feelings. We will judge on the basis of what is familiar in our experience, and expect it to be the same for him—and that is prejudice too.

Now supposing the person is close to us, and acts differently than we expect him to act. We are surprised or fearful or disappointed.

Self-giving love begins here with forgiveness. Forgiving difference, and the jolt of unexpected difference. Forgiving our own reactions. Taking a breath to calm the surprised feeling and the other feelings that crowd behind. Taking responsibility for our discomfort in our difference from the other person. Then coming away from the prejudgments to respect and trust for the other person's integrity.

A divorce because the person squeezed the toothpaste tube at the top instead of the bottom? If it weren't so devastating to the people involved it would be funny. But little irritations often focus larger problems.

Negotiation and accommodation can solve a lot of problems, like buying the top-squeezer his own tube of toothpaste. But even that won't answer a basic lack of forgiving. Forgiving is an attitude which goes much deeper into life than toothpaste. It can even cope with a husband's cheating or a wife's affair with a neighbor.

Forgiving love begins with the present, and goes on from there. The past remains and will be difficult to forget, but forgiveness doesn't hesitate to absorb the hurt. Because that is the reality about forgiveness. It takes the hurt, acknowledges the problem, accepts the person, and *loves in the direction of resolving the situation.*

Forgiveness is a two-way street. It may be that you are the one who needs to be forgiven for an act or an attitude. To be forgiven, you will need to be willing to renegotiate trust.

If you have wronged the other, it means choosing to change your actions and attitude. (The person who forgives you must be willing to see your words and acts as genuinely repentant.)

Then if you are to be genuine in the renewed relationship you will need to risk being yourself again. (The one who forgives you will have to trust you and risk being wronged again.)

That will mean being openly yourself without fear of hurting the other again. (And the one who forgives you must be open to a restored relationship without holding back.)

To repent is not to deny the past but to change your present direction. (To forgive is not to forget but to trust.)

Self-giving love does not demand acceptance but volunteers its repentance. (Self-giving love on the other hand does not withhold acceptance until repentance is volunteered.)

In any relationship where conflicts arise demands will need to be resolved—but there must be no demands *as conditions for repenting*. (And no demands as conditions for loving.) "I'll change if . . ." or "How can I love you when you're always . . ." are conditional demands for repenting and accepting which make it difficult for healing to take place.

Which of the following describe forgiving love?
_____ a. Being a doormat to let somebody walk over you

_____ b. Forgetting the injury done and erasing it from your memory

_____ c. Accepting the person and the hurt and trying to find a positive way of dealing with the break in your relationship

If you need to forgive someone, we must assume you already have "footprints" on you like a doormat. But forgiving does more than lie there in self-pity. It accepts the hurt and yet works at renewing the relationship that has been damaged, so (a) is incorrect—except you may feel like a doormat in the process! Neither is (b) correct, because it is functionally impossible to forget the injury done to you. Those who claim to "forgive and forget" have only buried the memory in some memory bank without dealing with the hurt. True forgiveness doesn't banish the hurt or try to ignore it but rather, as in (c), it accepts the person and the hurt and seeks a way through to a new and in many ways better relationship.

But what if a son—or daughter—doesn't earn your trust? What if your trust is betrayed? David Augsburger explores this in his book, *The Love-Fight.*

"I can't trust you anymore," parents often say. That's not true. The word "can't" is false. "I won't trust you anymore" would be a more honest statement.

"Can't" is an irresponsible word. It says, "Your actions make it impossible for me and I can do nothing—I am not responsible." When you change the words "I can't" to "I won't" the truth begins to surface bringing responsibility with it.

You might try something like this: "Yes, I trust you to use your best judgment. But I know from my own experience that one person's best judgment may not include quite enough important facts of knowledge to be completely dependable. And sometimes it may need buttressing with some help from others—even parents. If it's important to you that we trust you to use your best judgment, will you trust us to use our best judgment in the questions we raise and the suggestions we make?"

"I trust you." When I hear—or sense—that message from another person I feel loved, I feel accepted. I feel respected, I feel worthwhile.

"I don't trust you." When I receive that message from someone I love, I feel disliked, cut off, rejected.

Furthermore, when someone close to you says, "You don't trust me anymore," you may have to forgive what you do not yet understand. The person may be saying one of a number of things—

1. "I'm confused. I've just betrayed my own ideals. I've done things I'm ashamed of. Tell me that you trust me. I need a breath of trust."

2. "I'm angry. You talk about responsibility. But when I want to make a decision you insist on making it for me. I need to move, to breathe, to be me."

3. "I'm frustrated. You use your 'trust' to manipulate me. I feel your trust has too many strings attached like, 'I'll trust you if. . . .' Won't you trust my ability to choose what seems right to me?"

4. "I'm betrayed. You told me you trusted me, so I made the decision that seemed important to me. Now I see you don't respect me or my decision at all. You bear-trapped me. You led me to think I was free to choose, then snap. I'm caught and rejected."

5. "I'm guilty. I let you down, I admit it. But I need my quota of mistakes. If you expect me to be perfect— according to your standards—then 'trust' is the wrong word for our relationship. 'Obey' maybe, or 'copy,' but not trust."

Underline true or false.
a. True or false? To trust is to risk love on the behavior of another.
b. True or false? We only give trust to those who have shown they are trustworthy.
c. True or false? If I trust somebody I should not object to his behavior if I don't like it.

(a) True. (b) False. We trust future behavior, not past. (c) False. Trust has nothing to do with behaviors I might or might not like. We certainly should voice our objections to unacceptable behavior, but we don't object to the person.

Forgiving trust accepts the other person as he is and respects his right to be different.

But it also asks for trust in return. You can express your own feelings honestly and clearly as part of the process of resolving conflicts appropriately. The possibilities for you are here in eight trust behaviors.

1. *Avoid value judgments.* Instead of deciding the person is "untrustworthy" or "bad" or "indifferent," avoid all value judgments that commit the person to being bad or untrustworthy into the future. Be willing to forgive the past and trust his potential if nothing else.

2. *Object to behavior, not the person.* When a person does something you find objectionable, avoid prejudicial statements like, "You always . . . ." Instead, object to the behavior, not the person. "I don't like it when you. . . ."

3. *Risk yourself and your position.* If you are tempted to avoid a confrontation on behavior or hope that someone else might do it for you, remember Harry Truman's comment, "The buck stops here." Risk yourself and your position. Have an opinion and express it. Trust the other person not to cut you off.

4. *Be open, vulnerable.* Don't hide behind a mask or

maintain a safe distance when the other is hurting. Get alongside. Be open, vulnerable—you may be hurt too, but trust says, "I am with you, hurt me if you must, but I am with you."

5. *Use simple, honest statements.* Instead of threatening or manipulating the other person into doing what you want, use simple, honest statements and clear, open requests which will allow the other freedom to negotiate with you or rebut you.

6. *Make statements tentative.* When you do express an opinion or a viewpoint, don't be rigid or dogmatic. You may be wrong or misinformed. Make your statements tentative enough to be open to the other person's feelings. Instead of "This is the way it is," try "I believe the best way is. . . ."

7. *Allow room for spontaneous choice.* Avoid demands for absolute promises and ironclad guarantees from others. Allow room for spontaneous choices, responses, and actions.

8. *Respect other's freedom.* Within your responsibility to the other person (your child, your friend, your parent, your spouse) respect the other's freedom to think, to feel, to choose.

Here in summary are the trust skills:

1. Avoid value judgments.
2. Object to behavior, not person.
3. Risk yourself and your position.
4. Be open, vulnerable.
5. Use simple honest statements.
6. Make statements tentative.
7. Allow room for spontaneous choice.
8. Respect others freedom.

Now let's practice recognizing these skills.

"Keep your dreams for my future," your son says to you. "Slaving for forty years in the establishment only earns you a taste for tranquilizers. I want to quit school and start living." Which of the following are appropriate responses for you in this behavior? (Avoid value judgments.)

_____ a. "You're six kinds of a fool!"

_____ b. "I don't agree with your conclusions."

You may be feeling like telling him he's a fool but you'd better say it without the value judgment expressed in (a). Response (b) avoids judging him.

Suppose that your second instinct is to say, "We want you to stay in school because we expect you to make something of yourself." Which (one or more) of the following trust skills are being used?

_____ a. Risk yourself and your position.

_____ b. Use simple honest statements.

_____ c. Make statements tentative.

This is not a tentative statement because it lays expectations on the boy so you would not check (c). But it is reasonably honest in expressing those expectations (b) and to that extent you risk your position (a)—but not much!

Instead you say to him, "Suppose you quit school—what do you think you might do?" Which (one or more) of the following skills are being used?

_____ a. Be open, vulnerable.

_____ b. Allow room for spontaneous choices.

_____ c. Respect other's freedom.

This response is a trust statement since it includes all of the skills listed.

Then you raise another issue with him: "You say I'm a slave to my work. I guess there are times I've felt that way— but I also like what I'm doing. It's the kind of job I looked for, and trained for." Which of the following skills are being used?

_____ a. Avoid value judgments
_____ b. Risk yourself and your position
_____ c. Respect other's freedom
_____ d. Be open and vulnerable

Now you are opening the door to further expression of his viewpoints—a step toward understanding what is bugging him. This is a vulnerable position for some parents (d), and in revealing your feelings about the job means a risk (b). He might pick up what you say as an argument in his favor. But maybe he will see you as a person, and that is a step closer to understanding also.

There is a bit of value judgment in what you say at the beginning. The boy's statement, "Slaving for forty years in the establishment," may only be a general condemnation of society and not specifically directed to you. However, we often take things personally, as happened here.

While it may not appear obvious from the words, how you say all of this could give him the feeling that you respect his autonomy as a person (d).

Finally you say, "I want to appreciate your values whether I share them or not—but I think quitting school would be a mistake." Which (one or more) of the trust behaviors is involved?

_____ a. Avoid value judgments.
_____ b. Object to behavior, not person.
_____ c. Risk yourself and your position.
_____ d. Be open, vulnerable.
_____ e. Use simple honest statements.
_____ f. Make statements tentative.
_____ g. Allow room for spontaneous choice.
_____ h. Respect other's freedom.

Although the last part of the statement seems to shut the door on (g) and (h), spontaneous choice and freedom, it

> *wouldn't be appropriate to assume that we have to agree with everything a person does in order to show trusting behavior. You are avoiding a value judgment (a), and although you are objecting to a contemplated action, you are very accepting of the person (b). There seems to be an element of risk too (c) and certainly you are open and honest with yourself and with him, (d) and (e). And within the bounds of your opinion, you have been as tentative in your statement as you can be (f).*

Self-giving love starts on a foundation of forgiving and repenting. It works outwardly in attitudes of acceptance and trust.

In a situation of conflict you can encourage openness and trust by being open and trusting yourself. It involves the risk of being hurt or rejected, but risks are an important part of living. And if in risking and trusting you find your way to a finer relationship, you will have been amply rewarded.

Now add to forgiveness the skills of compassion, in the next chapter.

17
Skills of Self-Giving Love

B. Compassion: Discerns and Cares

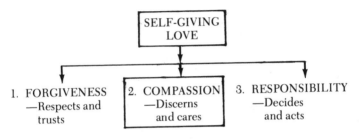

Compassion is feeling *with* another's problems and desiring to help. It attempts to discern the causes and drives and pressures which create tension and conflict. It *cares*.

Dr. Rollo May explains caring as a state in which something matters to you. It is the opposite of the apathy and cynicism which May labels as the besetting psychological illnesses of today.

There are at least three words which embrace the concept we are looking at here—care, concern, and compassion. In the intense emotions of conflict, I prefer the common meanings that the word compassion suggests: a feeling of sympathy and understanding for the hurt of the other.

To exercise this skill is to help the other person

through the conflict in a way that encourages his or her personal growth.

This calls for a discerning spirit, to sort out from your own feelings a sense of what the other person is reaching toward. Many of us have our minds made up on what the other person should be like, what they should be thinking, and how their character should be developing.

But this is *our* creation, and we need to stop playing God in the other person's life. We need to sift out our preconceptions so that we can begin to appreciate what is going on between God and the other person.

Then we can appreciate the other person's difference, without being threatened by it. And compassionate understanding of difference gives us a much better view of the other's growth.

All of us are growing or maturing—at least we ought to be. If I am willing to develop as God allows me the experiences to do it by, then I ought to allow others the freedom to mature also.

This doesn't mean closing my eyes to actions of the other person which I believe will hurt him. Not at all. That would be apathy and carelessness on my part. I will not stand by silently, but in taking the risk to challenge his behavior I must be compassionate. That calls me to discern his situation clearly from my own, and to care for his growth, my growth, and our relationship.

This aspect of self-giving love can be summarized in three practical behaviors—

1. *Learn to empathize with the other's problems or hurts.* This does *not* mean dropping your own opinions or feelings on the matter. Being understanding and compassionate won't make you a doormat for others to wipe

their feet on. It will make you a better person with a stronger personality. Yes, it will test your positions in a conflict. But if you compassionately try to discern the other's point of view, you will be stronger in your own view, if it is right for you—and it will be easier to change your position if you find it not worth holding.

2. *Develop the ability to set aside your own problems and situation* for the moment to see more clearly the other's difficulty. Most of us are so imbedded in our own life and its struggles that even when we seem to be compassionately listening—we are only remembering a similar situation that we've been through.

The skill is in learning to be objective. And in a highly emotional confrontation this is the last thing we want to do. We want the other person to be objective and compassionate toward us. Yet if you are sincere about trying to thread your way through all the debris of angry words and harsh feelings to a resolution, objectivity is a good vantage point in compassionate caring.

3. *Free yourself from the pressure of time.* Compassion needs time. Maybe you do have six other things to do yet today. And maybe you'll get in trouble for not completing your assignments. But if this person is important to you, you'll make time.

One husband-wife conflict that found its way to a marital counselor took a turn toward resolution when this was recognized. The counselor pointed out to the husband that although he said he felt compassion for his wife, the husband frequently checked his watch as she talked to him. In spite of his protestations that he cared, when he looked at his watch he was telling his wife that he wanted to move on to something "important" rather than to work through their conflicts.

For these compassion-caring behaviors fill in the blanks with one of the following words: (1) problems (2) time (3) ability (4) empathize

a. Free yourself from the pressure of _____.

b. Develop the _____ to set aside your _____.

c. _____ with the other's _____.

(a) time, (b) ability, problems, (c) empathize, problems

The following is an account of a telephone conversation between two friends, Alec and Bill, who have planned a vacation trip together for their families. As the conversation develops, Alec and his wife, Polly, use certain compassion behaviors. Can you identify them? In the blanks to the left of each set of italicized words indicate which (one or more) of the compassion behaviors listed below are in evidence:

    1. Empathize with the other's hurts.

    2. Set aside own problems.

    3. Take time to care.

Alec and Polly and the kids are having a late supper. Getting ready to leave in the morning has the children flying high—while Alec and Polly are beginning to drag. Then the phone rings—in the middle of supper.

____ a.   "It never fails," Alec mutters as he reaches for the phone. It's Bill, with a problem, "Hey, man, can't it wait? *We're in the middle of supper.*"

____ b.   He listens a moment, *then whispers to Polly, "Bill wants us to stay home tomorrow*—one of their kids has problems." Polly looks upset and responds, "But we promised the kids!"

____ c.   Alec listens as Bill has difficulty controlling his emotions. Finally Bill runs down and Alec says, "Hang in there, buddy, *I'll be right over.*"

____ d.   Instead Bill wants to come over with his wife and bring the child along. But Alec doesn't know what the situation is yet and he wonders what it will do to his own children. *He would prefer to find out*

first before throwing his family an unknown load.
____ e.   *"Bill, let me come over and talk* while Polly puts our kids to bed," Alec says. "Then maybe we'll get
____ f.   a sitter—or *we can all come back here and talk things over."*

The telephone is one of our modern conveniences, but why does it always ring at dinner time? In (a) Alec isn't showing much compassion for Bill—but he is trying to take time for his family (1). This may seem like a trick question, but it is important to recognize that difficult situations often involve the different needs of different people. In (b) Alec is beginning to discern Bill's hurt and empathize with him, so you likely marked it (1).

In (c) there is a mixture of compassion behaviors, (3) taking time and (2) setting aside dinner and plans for the evening. In (d) Alec is (1) empathizing with another problem: his children and his wife are a responsibility he must continue to consider. Then Alec reaches a decision to act for Bill and his family and for his own—and in (f) he (3) takes time, (2) sets aside his own problems, and (1) empathizes all around.

18
Skills of Self-Giving Love

C. Responsibility: Decides and Acts

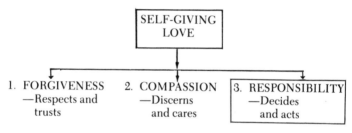

Self-giving love learns to forgive, to trust, and respect the other. Self-giving love compassionately discerns the other's hurts. It cares enough to understand and "weep with those that weep." And self-giving love *acts.* Responsibility searches out the path to resolution, makes decisions, and acts.

Love is the answer to conflict because of what it can bring to bear—understanding, sympathy, the integrity of self-love, objectivity, compassion, and *responsible action.*

Let's look at five behaviors you will need to make a part of your lifestyle in order to act with responsible love.

1. *Accept the responsibility of your own actions and feelings* which have influenced the conflict. It takes two to quarrel. You may feel that the conflict is all on the

other's side, and you may wonder why the other can't see and appreciate your point of view. But if there's a conflict, you can be sure there's something about your point of view or your attitudes that the other doesn't like. Accept that and go on from there.

2. *Make a long-term decision about your involvement.* Love doesn't vacillate or look for ways to duck out. Love says to itself, "I will do all I can from this moment on to resolve our conflict and improve our relationship."

Wenda Wordell Morrone and her husband, John, have been married six years—good, growing-together years overall. But it took basic commitments to overcome the adjustments each has had to make—even the simple one of geography. Wenda is from the rural Midwest, John from the metropolitan East. The commitment to marry involves the commitment to resolve differences and calls for the highest levels of responsible action. Wenda explains what it has meant to her:

"When you choose someone to marry . . . you make a public, bone-deep statement about yourself, putting a foot down in the direction you hope to head for all the time. . . .

"We're a unit, and we feel sure enough of that unit to be able to tinker with it without fear of shattering. It has something to do with the lack of time limits. I've gradually come to realize that one of the biggest assets of marriage is that it goes on as far as you can see into the future. . . . (so) we began thinking of long-term ways to behave, of overall problems—with each other, with the kids."

3. *Set reasonably attainable goals to work toward.* Discern what the problems are. Try to think of a course of action that might work toward solving the problem.

Don't drag up all the old battles you've had and expect to solve their problems along with your present conflict. Old conflicts ought to be left in the past—both of you have changed since then.

Be sure you understand. Then, forgiving yourself and your prejudices, start with accepting the other. Exercise all the compassion you can feel and muster up some more to add to it.

4. *Begin to act on your decision.* Make sure it is adequate and not just a token action to appear as if you are sincere. The action you choose may be simple or elaborate—as long as it works positively toward resolving the conflict.

5. *Check back with the person.* If your action begins to increase tensions you'll want to be sure that it is still working toward resolution and not making things worse. Remember the possibility that your conflict may heat up further in the process of being resolved.

Which statement seems a more appropriate description of the individual contributions to a conflict?
_____ a. Usually one person is right and the other person is wrong.
_____ b. There are two sides to every conflict and both persons have some responsibility for the tensions that exist.

It may be possible for one person to be right and the other wrong, but that is likely to be a rare occurrence. Far more likely—in fact almost universally so—is it that even the "innocent party" has contributed to the conflict. So answer (b) is more appropriate than (a).

In the situation below, Anne takes some responsible actions in trying to resolve tension in her relationship with a friend. Test your grasp of the responsibility behaviors summarized in the list below by trying to pick them out in the situation. In the blank spaces opposite the beginning of a sentence (or a sequence of sentences) write the numbers of one or more of the appropriate behaviors.

1. Accept responsiblity for your own actions and feelings.
2. Decide your long-term involvement.
3. Set reasonable, attainable goals.
4. Begin to act toward resolution.
5. Check the effect of your action.

_____ a. Anne felt she needed to do something to bridge the hurt between herself and her friend, Harriet.

_____ b. She hoped that Harriet would accept her earlier invitation to talk about their differences over lunch. She didn't expect Harriet to forgive her for being the reason Harriet had been transferred to a new department, not yet.

_____ c. First of all Anne needed to convince Harriet that she really didn't have a thing to do with it.

_____ d. Or did she? Anne wondered if the very fact that she had taken the course in consumer economics hadn't set the wheels in motion. She had prepared for the job. Harriet's promotion.

_____ e. So maybe she owed Harriet the honesty of admitting that much, although Anne hadn't thought of the consequences at the time.

_____ f. But she wasn't going to let Harriet's friendship slip away by not trying to mend fences. It would not be a quick and easy mending though because Harriet's transfer has hurt her possibilities for promotion.

_____ g. "Maybe I could help her take the course herself?"

_____ h. Anne dug out the college bulletin with the program in it. "I'm going to call her and see what she's decided about lunch."

Anne recongizes that, whatever has gone wrong, she is involved. She accepts her responsibility and is taking action.

So (a) is at least (1). Then in (b), Anne seems to have set herself a reasonable, attainable goal, and begun to act, so (b) can be (3) and (4). Anne, in (c), sets herself another goal (3) and while it may be difficult it's a goal she's willing to work at. Then she thinks about her own responsibility for the situation. Thus (d) is (1), and in (e) Anne accepts this also (1).

In (f), Anne decides her long-term commitment to Harriet's friendship, (2). In (g), she sets another goal (3) and begins another action (4). Finally she decides in (h) to check the effect of her original action with Harriet, (5).

Describe in your own words three of the five behaviors needed to act with responsible love.

A sufficient answer should include key ideas of at least three of the following:
   1. *Accepting responsiblity for your own actions and feelings.*
   2. *Making a long-term decision about your involvement.*
   3. *Setting reasonably attainable goals.*
   4. *Beginning to act.*
   5. *Checking back with the person.*

The conflict between Jesus and the religious leaders in Jerusalem increased with every confrontation. One of the experts in the law stood out of the crowd and tried to trap Him. "Teacher," he asked, "what must I do to be sure of eternal life?"

He asked the man, "What does the law say, and how do you interpret it?"

The man replied, "The law says, 'You shall love the Lord your God with all your heart and with all your soul and with all your strength, and your neighbor as yourself.' "

"Quite right," Jesus said, "Do that and you will live."

But the teacher of the law wanted to vindicate himself so he asked Jesus, "But who is my neighbor?"

Jesus replied, "A man was on his way from Jerusalem to Jericho when thieves stopped and mugged him, taking his clothes and everything of value, and leaving him half dead.

"It so happened that a priest came along, but when he saw the man he walked on by. The same for a Levite, who looked at the man then walked on by on the other side."

"But then a Samaritan traveler came along. (The Samaritans were despised by the people of Jerusalem and Jericho.) When he saw the wounded man his heart was filled with compassion. He treated his wounds and bandaged him. Then he put this man on this mule, took him to the nearest inn, and cared for him.

"The next day he gave the innkeeper some money. 'Take care of him, will you? If it costs more than I gave you, next time I come through I will give you the extra.' "

Then Jesus asked, "Which of these three men do you think was a neighbor to the thieves' victim?"

The teacher of the law answered, "The one who cared for him."

"Then you go and do the same," Jesus responded (Paraphrased from Luke 10:25-37).

Which of the following skills and behaviors did the Good

Samaritan seem to exhibit in caring for a man who could have been a traditional enemy?

       ____ a. Freed himself from time pressures

       ____ b. Set aside his own problems

       ____ c. Empathized with other's hurts

       ____ d. Accepted responsiblity for his own feelings

       ____ e. Made a long-term decision to be involved

       ____ f. Set reasonable goals

       ____ g. Began to act

       ____ h. Checked back with person

It is remarkable that the story Jesus told touches all of the compassion and responsiblity behaviors as thoroughly as it does. If you checked all of the above you are correct. The priest and the Levite were either too busy or afraid of getting involved. But the Good Samaritan interrupted his journey, set aside his own concerns, and perhaps in his empathy remembered all the times he might have been in the same trouble.

Further, while the priest and Levite likely felt sympathy for the man, only the Samaritan accepted responsibility for his feelings. He committed himself to the long-term involvement of caring for the man until his wounds were healed. He acted, within reasonable goals that allowed him to continue on his journey, planning to check back as soon as he could.

19
Self-Giving Love in Marriage

. . . What I do
And what I dream include thee, as the wine
Must taste of its own grapes. And when I sue
God for myself, He hears that name of thine,
And sees within my eyes, the tears of two.
—*Elizabeth Barrett Browning* in Sonnet VI of
Sonnets from the Portuguese

Elizabeth Barrett injured her spine in a fall from her horse when she was fifteen. During her long convalescence a lung ailment set in. This double curse doomed her to the life of a semi-invalid.

Robert Browning and Elizabeth Barrett shared the acclaim of nineteenth century enlightenment. Browning's *The Ring and the Book* placed him in the eyes of one critic as the greatest literary figure since Shakespeare. Yet Browning's singular achievement may well have been the sustaining love he gave to Elizabeth Barrett.

Elizabeth's father, Edward Moulton-Barrett, tyrannized his daughter's life. He demanded total obedience from his family and mostly got it. In her late thirties when Browning began to court her, Elizabeth never dared reveal to her father the extent of Robert's influence and affection. And when she made her decision to marry Robert Browning, Elizabeth was cut off completely by her father and never saw him again.

The Sonnets from the Portuguese are a collection of poems Elizabeth wrote secretly while Robert was courting her. There are few people who have not heard the sonnet which begins "How do I love thee? Let me count the ways. I love thee to the depth and breadth and height my soul can reach. . . ." The Brownings shared what has been regarded as a classic love for each other, and an example of what married love can be.

> And yet because thou overcomest so,
> Because thou art more noble and like a king,
> Thou canst prevail against my fears and fling
> Thy purple round me, till my heart shall grow
> Too close against thine heart, henceforth to know
> How it shook when alone. Why, conquering
> May prove as lordly and complete a thing
> In lifting upward as in crushing low:
> And as a vanquished soldier yields his sword
> To one who lifts him from the bloody earth,
> Even so, Beloved, I at last record,
> Here ends my strife. If *thou* invite me forth,
> I rise above abasement at the word.
> Make thy love larger to enlarge my worth.
> —*Elizabeth Barrett Browning*, Sonnet XVI

The crucible of marriage burns to a cinder many a love that is not love enough. What begins in physical attraction may never grow beyond sex to the relationship which sexual intercourse is meant to foster. And if this second level is not achieved there is no hope of moving into the third stage of mature fellowship in marriage which brings the happiest, loveliest years.

The error of the century began sometime in the fifties when advertising began to sell us *youth*. If you didn't connect with the great sex thing in your youth, then social and psychological destruction lay inevitably in wait. Age brought decay, not maturity, the error said. What happened in bed weakened by 30, dried up by 40, was unmentionable by 50.

There has also been admiration for sex without marriage. This second error suggested that in marriage a person might unnecessarily give up freedom and individuality.

So unencumbered sex was emphasized, the earlier the better, and if love developed out of sex, so be it. But time and reality have proven that sex without a foundation in love has little durability. The files of marriage counselors bulge with accounts of sex-turned-sour.

Turn the error over and talk of love and a different picture emerges. Marriages nurtured in love find sex does not dwindle in value as the years go by. On the contrary, many couples in their thirties, forties, fifties and beyond talk of a sexual experience much richer than in the traumatic years of early marriage.

So let's look beyond the television commercial's version of sexual love and see the reality of human experience. Married love begins in attraction, develops in relationship, and matures in fellowship.

True or false?
_____ a. Teenage marriages are more apt to succeed than later marriages.
_____ b. Marriage stands a better chance if you work at improving your relationship.
_____ c. A husband and wife can become "one" only if they give up their individuality.

(a) False. With all that youth has going for them, teenagers still seem unable to do as well in building a maturing relationship. (b) True. (c) False. In each partner self-love has a healthy identity to contribute to marriage— as two become one they couple their uniqueness for their mutual benefit, without losing their individuality.

1. *Love begins in attraction.*

Erotic love, according to Erich Fromm, craves complete fusion with one other person and is frequently confused with the lesser but often explosive experience of "falling-in-love."

"Falling-in-love" love is a disturbing and heart-wrenching compulsion of physical drives. David Augsburger describes this kind of love as *conditional*, earned by appearance, performance, and ability. If we can improve our looks and personality we may attract another and win approval. It is external and transient, surviving only as long as we live up to the other person's expectations and demands.

Yet mutual attraction is a nice thing to have going for you in marriage. It will always be a good idea for the husband to improve his skills as a courteous lover. Having won the girl's heart ten years ago he'd better not take her for granted now. Unfortunately, many a passionate Romeo has degenerated into an unsanitary slob. And many a beauty queen has diminished into ever-wearing hair curlers and slippers.

Attraction is a powerful spice to married life. And while it begins the dating game and urges us toward physical union, attraction in a good marriage never wanes.

Physical attraction is only part of it. We respond to other things we see in the one we are attracted to—or think we see. We project the possibility of the other person meeting our needs. (I need to feel important to someone, and she says I'm important to her.) We need to be needed and appreciated and we believe (or hope) the other can meet those needs.

We look for security too. Security against loneliness and rejection. Security in a world of mobility and change. And in the attractive other we see a defense against alienation and despair. In the security of the beloved we can risk adventure and enjoy change.

We expect the attractive other to meet these needs to our satisfaction. Yet our needs can only be fully realized in a developing marital relationship and maturing fellowship of love.

2. *Love develops in relationship.*

Marriage provides the structure for love's development. All of the behaviors and skills we looked at earlier have the possibility of working within the relationship of two becoming one. All the interest and variety of two individual characters shape a new entity called a "couple" or a "marriage."

Here the disciplines of responsibility find the time and the proximity and the occasion to develop. *Love can grow from attraction to relationship if we work toward a trusting, caring, responsible love*—not some hit-or-miss, let-love-happen-if-it-can romanticism. Marriage to succeed needs constant attention with all the skills of conflict resolution brought into play again and again and forevermore again.

The relationship of a growing marriage draws on what David Augsburger describes as internal love—love which honors, values, respects, and encourages the integrity of each partner.

It is love that calls forth love, giving to receive, and receiving to give again.

3. *Love matures in fellowship*.

"Practice makes perfect" is an old and reasonably reliable saying. Applied to marriage, there comes a time—soon or late—when the hard work of loving brings the glow of a new joy, a quality of companionship and understanding that can feed back into the relationship a source of added strength.

Rollo May calls it a relaxing in the presence of the beloved which accepts the other's being as being, and simply likes to be with the other. . . .

Wenda Marrone tells about a dreary dog-tired night spent comforting a sick child. Wenda began to cry and her husband, half-asleep, tottered in to see what was happening.

"I wearily waved him away. 'Go back to bed. Why should we both be awake? Anyway, you have to go to work in the morning.'

"John turned like a sleepwalker and shambled back to bed. When he was gone, self-pity set in. I really wept. . . . I was thinking . . . of the exhausting day that would follow, when the door opened. John stood there, only slightly more awake than before.

" 'I may not be able to help,' he said, 'but even if I just sit here beside you, I figure we're in this together.'

"It was a moment of solid gold. There have been others, and they make the romantic love I felt when I married seem lightweight by comparison."

These three phases in marital love are vital to the success of marriage:

1. Begins in attraction, and drives toward the two becoming one physically.

2. Develops in relationship, and drives toward security and stability as the two become "more one."

3. Matures in fellowship, and drives toward satisfaction of individual needs and goals as the two ultimately become intimately one.

There is no set calendar when these phases or stages begin. Some "marriages" never get beyond phase one. Some couples begin all phases at the same time. It might be considered normal for phase two and three to begin in the tentative exploration of commitment that we call "engagement". Then the couple, originally drawn together in mutual attraction, now agree to marry if they continue to feel about each other as they do.

What happens when "two become one?" If there is something going on in a marriage that is more binding than simply two people getting together to share sex, we should recognize it. Because, if this bond is developing, then divorce is a much more devastating experience than many of us admit.

The biblical concept of two becoming one has inspired many interpretations. Let's look at diagrams of four of these views.

1. Absorption

In marriage, one partner begins to absorb the weaker personality of the other. Not always is it the male absorbing the female; in many unions the wife dominates. This may better be called "one becoming none." Such a marriage succeeds only if what is happening suits both partners.

2. Overlap

In this popular view, the individuals are "one" in the area of overlap but retain their unique personalities outside of that area. Inasmuch as the couple give themselves to each other in the overlap, their bonding is secure.

3. Eternal Triangle

This concept includes God in the overlap. When God is invited into a marriage the bond is strengthened in a three-way tie of mutually shared experience. "Where two are together in my name, I am in their midst," Jesus said (Matthew 18:20). There is a problem in this concept and its "overlap" cousin. Both leave large areas of individuality outside the marriage. But marriage can include a sharing of the whole person, so that even individual pursuits can become benefits to the other partner.

4. Symbiosis

I prefer another view, *symbiosis*, which sees two individuals becoming one within the larger entity we call marriage or *union*. It is synergistic also in that the union is greater than the sum of its parts and seems to me to allow for full expression of both self-love and self-giving love. *Symbiotic union* then sees marriage as producing a larger-than-the individuals mutuality. Marriage in this view benefits from the retained individuality of each, yet produces a oneness which can have its own potential for growth. And where God is acknowledged, He can truly become Lord of all.

Identify the diagrams with their explanatory statements below by putting the correct diagram number in the space in front of each statement:

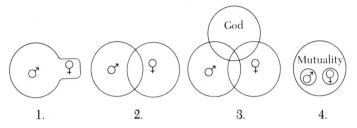

____ a. Shares commitment to each other while retaining some individuality outside of the mutual area.

____ b. God and each partner share an overlapping bond of commitment.

____ c. The marriage union becomes a fact in itself with possibility for growth through the mutual commitment and total sharing of the individuals.

____ d. A marriage where one person is largely absorbed by the dominant personality of the other.

Each of these views of "two becoming one" involves mutual commitment and sharing of personality. Diagram 2 fits statement (a). It tends to reserve an area of individuality separated from the partner and thus separated from the marriage commitment. Statement (b) applies to diagram 3, ag.iin tending to hold areas separate from each other and even from God. Statement (c) describes the symbiotic union in which individuality not only can but must continue in order to add all its vitality to the union which grows larger-than-life through the total commitment of both to each other and to God.

Diagram 1 applies to statement (d) in the shrinkage of one personality in an absorbing relationship.

Self-giving love strengthens marriage as it strengthens all our relationships, without diminishing the individual. In fact, it seems to be a law of the human personality that the more we give of ourselves, the more there is to give. This law has its inverse side too, in that if we withhold love in ourselves, our ability to love withers and disappears.

In the heightened tensions of conflict, self-giving love is the necessary base for achieving the mutual satisfaction of conflicting needs while actually strengthening the relationships.

Part IV
Confronting Your Problem

20
Knowing Your Feelings

"Then throw off falsehood; speak the truth to each other. . . . If you are angry, do not let anger lead you into sin; do not let sunset find you still nursing it; leave no loop-hole for the devil" (Ephesians 4:25-27, NEB).

In part one we saw how people react to conflict in five common ways. In part two we explored the ways we communicate with each other and how that affects conflict. Then when we looked at the strength of self-giving love in part three we saw how our attitudes and motivations could influence the outcome of our conflicts.

Now, in part four, we will begin to bring together the basic skills of communication and the will to love as we deal with the head-on collisions of conflict.

Most of us have picked up our "combat training" in school and neighborhood—and home. Likely what we have learned in the past hasn't helped us much at all. Too often when a quarrel starts, reason flees. Emotions rise up and take over. The tactics for defense we learned on the street and which have become our way of quarreling move in and we go on automatic. We say things we regret. We hear things we hang onto for the next battle.

We brood and ache and rehearse devastating arguments to support our position.

In the meantime we have done little to improve our abilities to handle conflicts. In fact, each conflict tends to mire us deeper in our methods and our pain, unless. . . .

Unless we discover a better way. And there is a better way. We *can* alter how we handle our emotional responses. And by the grace of God the direction of our conflict-seared lives can be changed.

"Trading for this car was your stupid idea," your wife says angrily. "Now we're stuck with a lemon."

"That's not true," you counter. "We bought the one *you* wanted."

"I really was happy with the old car," she says. "And I think you let the salesman talk you into this one because you wanted it."

You turn the key again and the starter whines but the motor still doesn't catch.

"You've been had," she digs. "But you won't admit it."

You twist the key again like you wish it were her ear. She talked you into thinking the old car was getting too old, then blames you for trading. But maybe you bought this particular model just to show her she should leave these decisions to you? And if it had turned out right you could keep her in her place?

This is the way it always seems to go, blame and counter-blame. And either way, you're both being had in these no-win battles. It has bothered you for a long time. Somebody has to make a move for honesty. And for a new direction.

"Jill," you say, "we're getting further apart every time

we fight. You're out to win by blaming me. I'm out to win by putting you down. We both lose. Right now I don't care who wins. I just wish we could be close again."

Her surprised look lasts only for a moment, then gives way to thoughtfulness as she nods.

"I guess that's really what I want, too," she admits. Then with a rueful smile she adds, "and I wish I'd said it first."—David Augsburger in *The Love-Fight* (adapted)

The main idea in part four is to discover the ability to understand and to express your primary feelings clearly in such a way that the other person can respond openly with his—as you move in the direction of resolving your conflicts.

This is the basic skill in confronting your problem. You confront your feelings—and his—with honesty and integrity. And so in part four we will look at the skills in identifying your primary and secondary feelings. We can then see the importance of who owns which part of the problem. Following this we will look at several ways our emotional drives are expressed, including how far we should go in opening up our feelings to others.

And we will take a special look at the values—and dangers—of anger. We will explore how to recognize responsibility for anger and what we should do about it.

Following that you will begin to learn the skill of communicating your feelings, your needs, and expectations in clear "I messages." We will look at the differences between "I" and "you" messages and how they affect conflict.

Then you will try the skill of helping the other person define his problem and express his feelings through active listening.

Finally we will look into the problem of the impossible situation, when no one will move because no one wants to—and we will see how you might make the impossible possible.

Ed Dayton is executive director of MARC, Missions Advanced Research and Communications Center, a division of World Vision.

"It was a strange thing," Ed writes in a MARC Newsletter editorial. "I never went out of the way to make people like me. I just assumed they would. After all, I was a right thinking, clean living, professionally skilled person. Who wouldn't like me?

"Perhaps the first rude awakening came when we moved to Grand Rapids. One of our earliest friends here was a delightful couple—Lois and Caryll Rawn. The first time we were together we picked them up to take them to some kind of meeting or concert. . . . I don't even remember what [we talked about], but I was holding forth on it in my usual positive and authoritive way.

"During the coming weeks Lois and [my wife] Marge became good friends, and eventually Lois was able to share with Marge that [I] scared her half to death. What had I said? How had I acted? I had no idea. But as I began to look around for other signs of the same phenomena, I discovered there were other people that really were scared. I didn't mind *engineers* who didn't like me. That was part of the professional game. But to have a lovely, warm person like Lois Rawn not like me, or at least to be frightened of me, was shattering.

"I still find I want people to like me. I suppose that's a perfectly natural human desire, and I would be surprised if it isn't shared by most of the human race. What really surprises *me* is that it took me so long to discover that there just might be people who didn't like me.

"So began my journey into an exploration of what love is all about. It's taken me a long time. I'm still learning, I'm not sure whether it's feeling (yours or mine), whether it's just action, or whether it just deals with total acceptance. . . .

"My wife is helping both as a subject and object of love. 'Husbands, love your wives, as Christ loved the church. . . .' That's almost an incomprehensible statement, but she makes it seem possible.

"My friends are helping me too. . . . The Lord works in mysterious ways, but most always through people. . . . I'm sure He knows what He's doing, but I wish He'd turned His troops loose on me twenty years sooner!"

Ed Dayton is fortunate. He has discovered how some people feel about him and his ways. Yet for years he didn't know people were afraid of him, even his friends. Like Ed Dayton's friends, we find it terribly difficult to tell another person how we feel, face to face.

We can talk about another person, but not about each other. For instance, I won't have much trouble at all telling you how my friend felt last week about his boss. In fact if he had a round with him I'll *enjoy* telling you all about it.

Move it a little closer and I won't be quite as comfortable telling you how *I* feel about my friend and something he did that bothered me last week. And I'll be less comfortable telling you how I feel about him right now. Even more difficult will be to tell you how I felt about *you* last week. Finally it'll be downright awkward telling you how I feel about you right now. It is relatively simple *talking about others and my past feelings* toward them. It is very difficult *talking to you about my present feelings* toward you here and now.

According to John L. Wallen in *Developing Effective Interpersonal Communication*, we are afraid of our feelings. Our inability to handle emotions is the most frequent source of strain in our relations with others. When differences arise we experience strong feelings but we aren't able to identify clearly why we feel the way we do, nor what we should do about them. And as Wallen points out, we are uncomfortable with the strong unexplained feelings of the other person.

Consequently we have learned to fear and distrust our feelings. And we deny or ignore our feelings, hoping to deny or ignore their effect upon our conflicts.

It is easier to tell you what I really think about you than to tell you about a friend. True or false?

False. Because we haven't learned how to express our feelings, particularly in a conflict, we usually find it easier to gossip about another person. And since gossip, like rumor, is rarely accurate or complimentary, it is one "skill" we can do without.

True or false? Emotions should be kept under control and even submerged in a conflict, or we risk making things worse.

False. Unfortunately most of us act as if this were a good idea. But again, because we have not learned to identify our feelings and express them clearly, we squelch them in tight-minded control—or let them explode like shrapnel in all directions. Most of us choose the first alternative and learn to bury our feelings, until we lose touch with some of them altogether.

It has been said that *emotions* are the energies we use in perceiving an experience, and that *feelings* are the descriptions—verbal or physical—we give to our emotions.

Unfortunately, our descriptive feelings may not come across clearly. When I walk down to the corner to pick up the paper, I may whistle. You can't tell by my whistle whether I'm delighted with the weather or distracted by worry. If we pass and I say, "Nice day, isn't it," and you agree, it may still not mean either of us is aware of the weather. Or even—if someone should ask—aware of our feelings.

In a quarrel your emotional temperature may reach the point that you yell, "Shut up!" You are communicating anger by your eyes and the tone of your voice. But inside you may be experiencing frustration at too many confusing elements the other person is throwing at you. Or you may simply hurt so much you don't want to hear more.

When a special weekend back home comes around and you are "up on cloud nine" you are probably elated for several emotional reasons: happy relief at not having to face usual weekend activities, happy anticipation at the trip to your relatives, happy warmth in the relationships that will be renewed, happy excitement at the games and activities you will all enjoy.

It is not likely to be very important to separate out why you are happy at an anticipated weekend with your folks. But when you yawn in a conversation with your wife it can be devastatingly important to find out whether you are just tired or you're bored with your life together and not doing anything about it.

Now, for an exercise in feeling, look around the room

you are in. Are you warm enough? Too warm? Is the chair pressing up under your legs? The muscles in the back of your neck—are you tense?

How do you feel about your day? Has it been good? So-so? A drag? Why do you feel that way about it? Who influenced you most to feel that way about today? Can you identify why that person made you feel good or bad? Can you analyze the several different shades of feeling?

How do you feel, now that you have been reminded of today? Is your neck as tense or more so? You have likely forgotten how you felt a moment ago about the temperature in the room, or about your chair.

Feelings often happen to us before we are aware of what has caused them. A man you meet at the barbecue begins to make you feel embarrassed, then you realize he is talking a little too loudly. But the real reason for your discomfort is that he is passing on some unflattering gossip about the host who is almost within hearing distance.

One of the confusing things about emotions and feelings is that they show up in different expressions. As the man's story about the host gets louder, your wife may begin to look nervously at you, signaling with her eyes, "Do something." You may begin to pull at your shirt collar because you don't seem to be getting enough air. Your wife is rubbing her hands together. You feel hot in your face. Your smile is pasted on and fading.

These are physical reactions and your body is speaking its feelings in response to the storyteller's words. What about inner demands? Later your wife tells you she was afraid you were going to tell the man off—then she became angry that you didn't. You tell her about the inner confusion you experienced and how you just wanted to find a chance to change the subject. "Because," as you explain, "all that party needed to ruin it for everybody was for me to tell that guy off!"

You were embarrassed in this situation. Suppose someone else felt another way—perhaps angry or bored or amused or even entering into the situation with a story himself. Let's look at how various feelings of different people might have been expressed, physically and verbally. Note the variety in verbal expressions, describing either feelings themselves or the actions urged by the feelings. Note also the kinds of avoiding statements which lie about our feelings, perhaps to keep them in check to our disadvantage.

Anger—Muscles tense. Face gets red, mouth sets. "I want to hit you," reports the action you feel toward the loud-voiced gossip. Or you can clearly express your deeper feelings, "I don't like hearing a story like this about a friend when he isn't here with us."

Avoiding: "Why don't you shut up?" This is a "you-message" which fails to communicate your feelings clearly. Instead it demands an action from the other which is apt to create additional tension.

Amusement—Suppose the story about your barbecue host is harmlessly amusing rather than embarassing. Then your eyes may shine, mouth opens, lungs push out air. "That makes me laugh," reports your physical response. Feelings say, "I feel good—has he heard that story himself? Let's get him over here."

Avoiding: "It takes a better story than that to make me laugh" may suggest you have repressed your ability to be amused. Perhaps in the past you laughed when it was inappropriate, and now you'd rather be safe than sorry.

Sympathy—Suppose the story is about a loss your host has suffered. Then your face may frown, eyes soften, head tilt. "I could cry," reports how you might like to act. Feelings: "I am deeply moved by what I hear."

Avoiding: "That reminds me of the time. . . ."

Boredom—Nothing turns you on at this party, especially the gossip. So here comes the big yawn, covered politely with your hand, as you look at your watch. Feelings might say, "I'm getting dull and tuning out what you're saying."

Avoiding misstatement: "Say, it's getting late."

In the first example, "Embarrassed" tried to change the subject in his avoiding technique as the storyteller gossiped about his host. How much more comfortable he would have felt for the rest of the evening *if he had expressed his feelings and needs honestly.* But most of us will put up with discomfort and inner conflicts in our principles rather than speak our feelings and risk a scene.

And this is probably not an unreasonable price to pay at times for social stability. In certain circumstances "tact" or "politeness" may call upon you to ignore certain behaviors and make the best of them. It is one thing to put up with a bore or a gossiper at a barbecue— quite another if the bore calls you every day on the phone, or the gossip turns into malicious and character-destroying lies.

> True or false?
> _____ a. We often become angry or despondent or happy before we are aware of the cause.
> _____ b. Our feelings are revealed by our words.
> _____ c. It is more important to keep the peace than to reveal our feelings.

As we will see later, anger usually has another feeling behind it—jealousy or fear or disappointment. The same is true of happiness or despondency. Feelings are complex stirrings within us, and what we express on the surface may be different than what we feel inside. Item (a) is true.

Item (b) is false. Often our words disguise what our gestures or facial expressions reveal more accurately.

In (c), like the illustration of the storyteller at the party, it depends somewhat on the story he is telling. When we are personally involved in a conflict it is important to identify and express our feelings—but in a way which will help to resolve the conflict (more on this later). So you will likely have marked false.

How open should we be with our feelings? Only as open as the situation requires. For some people who are clamshells, that is likely to be more open and honest about their feelings than they've been for years, perhaps since childhood. For others who are apt to unbutton themselves and their feelings to uncaring strangers, it means establishing some guidelines for self-disclosure.

For our purposes here, the process first begins with being open and honest *with ourselves*. As we become accustomed to understanding our feelings, then we should express them when doing so (1) will help the other understand what is happening to us and (2) will encourage a wholesome relationship.

On the other hand we should not force our feelings on the other when those feelings make inappropriate demands upon his freedom or integrity.

The attitude which governs the kind of feelings which are appropriate for us to share is part of the teaching of the New Testament, as in the following paraphrase of the letter from the Apostle Paul to the Christians at Ephesus (Ephesians 4:25-32):

"Don't lie to each other but speak the truth; remember we are really part of each other. If you become angry don't let it get the best of you, but deal with it right away, otherwise you give the devil a chance to make things worse. . . .

"Do not let your mouths speak unwholesome thoughts, but speak only what will help reconcile the situation, words which God can use to encourage those who hear. Never grieve the Holy Spirit of God whose purpose works reconciliation in us and marks us for the day of redemption.

"So let there be no bitterness and rage, no more destructive blaming or malicious slander. Instead be compassionate with one another, reaching for understanding. Be ready to forgive each other as God in Christ forgave you."

When is it appropriate to share feelings? When is it unwise? In the following situations mark A (appropriate) or X (unwise):

_____ a. You are traveling on a bus and the stranger beside you invites you to share confidences.

_____ b. You are in a group of friends and one person wants to tell about an affair she's had with one of the men in the group.

_____ c. Your husband is sensitive about something that has happened on a business trip and you suspect he's feeling guilty about it. Should he tell you?

_____ d. Should you tell him your suspicions? Ask him to share?

(a) *Unless the confidences the stranger wishes to share are relatively innocent, you likely will not feel comfortable in this situation and will mark this (X). Openness and honesty is not a matter of how much of your past history is plain to others, but the quality of person you are now. And how honest you can be in your relationship now.*

   (b) Open disclosure of such intimacies in a group can be a device to get revenge or involve others or seek justification for actions. The value of such open specific confession is questionable unless the group is unusually and exceptionally mature in its abilities to encourage forgiveness and reconciliation. You will likely mark this (X) also.

   (c) Confession and forgiveness is much more appropriate within the limits of those who may need to confess and forgive, so you will have marked this (A). If the husband needs to ask his wife's forgiveness he should reexamine his motives and intentions so that he is also making his recommitment to the future health of their relationship. And above all he must not confess simply to shift his burden of guilt to his wife.

   (d) If you have suspicions it will be much more appropriate (A) to share than to harbor them—but in doing so, you will need to be ready to soak up some hurts—and forgive.

We are being deceived about life if we live on the surface without knowing and taking counsel with our emotions. But if we allow ourselves to feel—if we discover that we *do have* feelings about the many experiences through which we pass each day—our lives will take on new and richer flavor. And we will be better prepared to deal with our conflicts.

How often have you wished for a replay of an argument so that you could say what you really meant, instead of what you did say? The process of the conflict helped you to see your own needs more clearly. Now that you know what you want, you wish you had the opportunity to back up and start again.

Let's say two things here. One, there is no reason why you can't ask the other person for a replay. You might explain, "About what we said to each other, I'd like to back up and start over. I've had some entirely new insights since then that will change the direction of what we said."

Second, if you practice knowing yourself and how you feel about things that relate to you and the other party, you may succeed in expressing yourself more satisfactorily the first time.

Again we come back to the problem of knowing ourselves and our feelings. Through pressures at home and at school as we developed, we are apt to think of ourselves in stereotypes. We admire one of our acquaintances and try to take on some of the admired characteristics. Some kids try to be like their parents—while others try hard *not* to be like their parents.

So in the process of trying to be like—or not to be like—someone else, we develop an idea of who we are that may be far from the real personality hiding somewhere behind our self-portrait.

In her book, *The Brother's System for Liberated Love and Marriage*, Joyce Brothers suggests a simple method for getting better acquainted with yourself. Make a list of five things you really want out of life more than anything else. This won't be easy. As the author points out, it takes some people several weeks to be able to think through all the superficial wishes in order to get to the real core of what they would like to accomplish. You will probably tear up a half-dozen lists before you come close to knowing the person that you really are.

The purpose in better knowing who you are is to help you define the needs you feel in a conflict. Remember three of the styles of conflict? WITHDRAW gives up on relationships as well as on attaining personal needs.

YIELD gives up on needs in order to maintain the relationship. And RESOLVE attempts to achieve most of the needs of both as well as to improve on the relationship in the process.

Conflict involves the clash between two persons or parties whose drives toward fulfilling their needs run up against each other. It is normal to have needs, to want to achieve certain goals. It is also normal to be frustrated at some point along the way by the conflicting needs of another.

In the process of resolving the conflict, the first step is knowing clearly your need and what must be done to fulfill it. The clearer this is to you the easier it will be to make adjustments, when blocked by another's needs, in order to get to where you both must go with the least amount of disruption.

We can summarize it this way:

1. My basic need is _____.

2. I see it working out this way _____.

3. But if our needs clash, I can rearrange mine like this _____.

If you can get ahold of your side of the conflict in this way, you're in good shape. But that won't happen to you in the middle of an argument. And that's why self-preparation can be so helpful.

Remember what your RESOLVE is working toward:

1. To satisfy as much as possible of the needs of both of you.

2. To benefit and improve your relationship.

To this basic definition of the RESOLVE style we have added—

3. To help each of you grow in a healthy way through the experience.

This last item needs to be clearly a part of your RE-SOLVE or else it is self-defeating. Without both of you growing in a good way, you're no further ahead at all.

A good way to get to know yourself is to ask somebody else to describe you. True or false?

This could be a way to get a new insight into your personality, if the other person knows something about you that you haven't seen, so if you answered True for that reason you're on target. Another way might be to try to list five things you want most out of life. Not so much in the hope you might get what you want, but that in the process you see more clearly your personality.

While you make your list, it would be good to look at God's description of a well-rounded person in the New Testament, particularly in Paul's letter to the Roman Christians (Romans).

The value of knowing your needs clearly is (check one or more of the following):
_____ a. Being able to express them well
_____ b. Being sure nobody interferes in achieving them
_____ c. Being able to negotiate their achievement during conflict

Item (a) is certainly one of the advantages of knowing your basic needs in a situation. But not so you can achieve them at all costs (b)! In working toward a resolution, (c) knowing your needs is important.

Now, having determined to know who you are and what you feel, there's another problem every conflict gets into on the level of feeling: the problem of anger. Let's look into it in the next chapter.

21
The Problem of Anger

"The light turned green," Bill said, "and I started across the intersection. But out of the corner of my eye I saw a car coming down the hill too fast to stop.

"I pulled the wheel over hard and hit the brake at the same time. He swung away from me and I managed to turn parallel with him. That was too close for comfort! I just sat there and twitched—while the other guy pulled around and headed off up the street. That's when I laid on the horn at the stupid jerk."

Anger is worth taking a look at by itself in this chapter. It is a complex emotion, useful at times, destructive at other times. As a useful drive it can move people to heroic deeds against evil and evil men. For instance Ralph Nader and his Raiders have been called "angry young men" because of their determined work to reform American business practices.

Thomas Gordon calls anger a secondary emotion. In his book, *Parent Effectiveness Training*, Gordon describes anger as something generated solely *after* the experience of an earlier primary feeling such as disappointment, frustration, or fear. Furthermore, as a secondary feeling, anger almost always becomes a "you-message" which communicates judgment and blame.

While anger is nonetheless real and a powerfully upsetting experience, Gordon suggests people make themselves angry to impress the other person and change his behavior. It's an act to show him what he has done, or to teach him a lesson and convince him he shouldn't do it again. For instance, in the story at the beginning of the chapter, the man who avoided the accident was first frightened, then became angry as a means of punishing the driver so he would be more careful in the future.

Psychologist Fritz Perls sees anger as warm and constructive or cold and destructive. Cold annihilating rage seeks to destroy obstacles or remove frustrations. Warm anger blends frustration with expression of needs and can lead to creative resolution.

Psycholgist Arnold Buss believes that anger can become an enduring inner attitude of hostility through a process of labeling or categorizing.

Psychoanalyst Erich Fromm describes aggression as either benign or malignant, socially learned or biologically rooted. Biologically rooted aggression is useful in meeting basic human needs for survival and achievement. Malignant aggression emerges from personal predicaments which can distort character or foster violence.

For the moment, let's say anger is an emotion we must learn to live with, understand, and allow to work only in appropriate behaviors.

Another translation of the Apostle Paul's words to the Ephesian Christians we looked at in the last chapter begins, "Finish then with lying and speak every man the truth with his neighbor. For we are members one of another." Paul applauds the way of being candid and open with each other. We cannot afford lies or cover-ups if we are to build and maintain good relationships.

Paul then urges them, "Be angry, but sin not." He defines sin as the violation of relationships. Sin in my life is the choice I make either to live without you in withdrawal, against you in hostility, over you in superiority, under you in dependency, or in spite of you in rejection or indifference.

In managing our anger, we need first to admit to ourselves that we are angry and to reach into ourselves for its cause. "I am angry. I am feeling a deep demand to change whatever has caused my anger."

Second, we can then turn the anger we feel to creative relationship-building rather than to destructive ends that push people away. Mismanaged anger violates relationships, and that is the sin Paul warns us to avoid. "Be angry, but sin not," or "If you become angry don't let it get the best of you."

Check which (one or more) of the following statements about anger seem to be the most appropriate:
_____ a. Anger is always a destructive emotion.
_____ b. Anger can become a characteristic of personality.
_____ c. Anger toward another person should be expressed clearly to the person.

Anger in some of its forms can be a positive drive for aggressive, constructive action if it is recognized and used in positive, relationship-building concern. If you checked (a) as appropriate, you will want to review the descriptions of anger, particularly that of Fritz Perls and Erich Fromm.

Statement (b) is appropriate when you consider that internalized anger can produce personalities soured with hostility and destructive aggression. Our personalities now are the result of the direction we have been growing in. If we are hostile or withdrawing or intense or accepting, we tend to add to these and become more hostile or more accepting.

And simply expressing our anger (c) clearly has little benefit, if we are not sure why we are angry. If as Thomas Gordon points out anger is a secondary emotion, then we need to understand the demands of feelings that lie behind our anger. These demands may be important to us and it is these which should be clearly expressed, instead of just the anger.

Fill in each blank with one or more of the following words.

a. Demands of feelings	d. Relationships
b. Calmly	e. Immediately
c. Personality	f. Despair

1. Mismanaged anger violates ＿＿＿＿＿＿＿＿.
2. The first step in dealing with anger is to identify the

＿＿＿＿＿＿＿＿.

3. Anger should be dealt with ＿＿＿＿＿＿＿＿.

If we do not handle our anger suitably we will likely do harm to our relationships (d) with others. We may also violate personality (c),our own or the other person's, so either word would be suitable in (1).

In (2), since our anger is likely a secondary feeling, we need to get inside it to the demands of our feelings (a) in order to clearly understand why we feel as we do.

And while it may seem wise for us to deal with anger calmly (b) that is likely to be not quite as important as dealing with it immediately (e), before it festers and becomes a larger hostility than we can handle.

In a *Gospel Herald* article David Augsburger points out that anger can rise above sin and be constructive "when it seeks to break through the barriers between us—at least the barriers for which I have responsibility. If I deal with aggression constructively I can remove barriers by affirming clearly, 'I'm frustrated with the distance between us,' 'I want to be close again,' ' I want to experience understanding and community.'

"For example," Augsburger explains, "I find when counseling husbands and wives that to encourage them only to express their anger to each other is a waste of their time and mine.

"But to encourage them to own the feelings of anger that move within them and to begin to define what they are demanding of each other is very helpful. Then each has the opportunity to deal with a clearly defined demand—the barrier between them—instead of a vague, unclassified resentment."

22
"I" and "You" Messages

"Jed was mad at me for something," Colleen explained. "It was more than just some little thing, but I couldn't understand what was bugging him. When I asked him to tell me what was wrong, he said nothing was wrong at all.

"But there was, I could tell. He had a quietness about him, you know? A person can feel it when someone else is holding back. We just weren't having the easy time together we'd been having. Instead Jed was getting quieter and more like he didn't want to talk except about ordinary things, like where he'd put his car keys.

"It got so bad one weekend I couldn't take it any longer. He said something, nothing really, and I started to cry—I couldn't help it. He started to go out, and I wouldn't let him. I stood in front of the door and told him he'd have to hurt me to move me and I wanted to know what it was I'd done or was doing that he didn't like."

Colleen finally got to the point of confronting Jed— let's heave a sigh of relief! Now we'll hear from Jed.

"I shouldn't have let it build up in me, but for a while I hardly knew what it was that bugged me. By the time I figured it out, I was just plain ornery enough to figure she kept doing it to make me sore.

"I'd pick her up at her job on the way home from work bone tired, but she'd run her mouth about all the flak she got from customers. Some days all the way home. All through supper. One nonstop gripe. It got on my nerves."

Let's look at Jed-the-sullen and his problem

1. Isn't he being an irrational slob? To blame her for doing it to make him angry?

2. Just like most of us, Jed let himself build a little irritation into a mountain of rejection.

3. Why didn't he confront Colleen with his need to back off from the pressures of the day and talk small-talk while he unwound?

4. And if he couldn't offer sympathy, why didn't he challenge Colleen's gripes in a way that might help her survive the customer flak without pulling him down?

But such is the stuff of broken relationships. Little straws of hostility that build up a backbreaking load of antipathies and antagonisms. Now let's see how confronting might have worked.

Colleen does finally confront Jed with a last-ditch stand at the front door. As mean and miserable as they both feel at that moment, it's even money Colleen will pick up a fat lip and Jed a scratched eye. But supposing Jed catches the hurt in her tears and the desperation in her voice? She is asking for openness from Jed. She risks being hurt more if Jed ignores her or evades the question.

Worse, he could pretend as he has been doing that there's nothing wrong. He could cover up and tell her he loves her, ask why she's getting upset over nothing. But that would be patching a growing wound with a Band-

Aid of false and momentary warmth.

A lot of us do that sort of thing. We avoid: "Surely you're kidding, Colleen—what's for supper?"

Or we placate: "I'm sorry. Have I been making you feel bad? What a terrible thing to do!" Recognize the YIELD strategy? Or we shout the other person down in true WIN style, "You're out of your skull, woman. Shut up and let me out the door before I deck you."

But the need here is for Jed to level with Colleen. She has invited an honest, clear statement like this from Jed: "I'm tired when I pick you up from work and then I get a load of grief from your job dumped on me that I haven't the strength or the inclination right then to handle."

He's saying what he feels. He's still blaming her a little and there's a disguised "you dump a load on me every day" which blames her for his anger. It would have been better to explain: "I'm tired when I pick you up and I don't like the struggle right then of dealing with tensions I feel from your job."

That's an "I-message" which is considerably different in effect from a "you-message." "You-messages" throw the burden of the whole problem back on the other person. "You start griping about your work as soon as you get in the car. You make me angry." Or "Why can't you handle your own job and its problems? Why do you dump them on me?"

"You messages" obscure the underlying causes of conflict. When I blame *you* for my anger, then I'm saying, "Your action caused my anger. Now you must act to make me feel right again."

In effect I give you power over my reactions and I will hold my anger toward you until you meet my demands. I give you power to please me or to keep me angry and I am powerless to deal with my own reactions. I must wait on you to ease my anger. I am unable to be me, and by imposing on you the burden of healing my hurts, I won't let you be yourself either.

But if I recognize that *I* make me angry, then what you do does not control my reaction. I am responsible for my preceptions and feelings and what I will do about them.

"I messages" help clear the air as to who owns the problem. Jed blamed his anger on Colleen but Jed could have reacted with sympathy, so his brooding anger was *his* problem.

Let's look at another couple. Perry and Wilma, in their mid-forties, with children 19, 16, and 15. The oldest and youngest seemed normal and well-adjusted, but 16-year-old Bruce gave them fits. According to Wilma the boy left his room in a mess, wouldn't take a bath every day, and ignored her when she spoke to him about it. On the other hand Bruce insisted his room suited him fine, and he saw no reason to shower every day. "I'll shrink with all the wrinkles," he said.

Wilma badgered Perry to correct the boy, insisting that her husband stand with her. Perry attempted to discipline Bruce, even helped him to clean up his room. Wilma objected to this as letting the boy get away with his rebelliousness. At this point Perry defended Bruce as "just going through a phase" and a serious quarrel erupted.

Whose problem is this? Bruce doesn't seem to have had any to begin with, although he certainly has one now with a fight going between his parents over his conduct.

Perry didn't have a problem with Bruce's messiness

until he (1) took up Wilma's cause and attempted to correct Bruce and (2) then failed to satisfy Wilma's demand.

Wilma had the problem to begin with. She didn't like the mess. ("I have to clean this house, you know.") She didn't like a break in the routine of daily baths she had long assumed were next to godliness. She had attempted to make her problem Perry's as well as Bruce's. When Bruce refused to accept her standard any longer, she turned it on her husband. When he vacillated she felt she must stand her ground and get things straight with Perry and with her son.

Perry could have helped his wife in a number of ways. Of the statements below which (one or more) do you think are the most appropriate action Perry should take?

_____ a. He should set up a program of incentives for Bruce to encourage him to change to meet the family standards.

_____ b. He should simply tell Bruce to "shape up or ship out." Kids need discipline, particularly today, and Perry should demand obedience from the boy, to teach him the kind of treatment he's going to run into in the real world.

_____ c. Perry should challenge his wife to revise her standards and maybe give Bruce some room to grow in.

_____ d. Instead of accepting Wilma's idea that he should back her in a united front against Bruce, Perry should help Wilma see that she is a unique person with her own standards that may or may not coincide with his.

_____ e. Perry could say, "You're always nagging me to do your dirty work. Why don't you tell him yourself?"

_____ f. Perry could confront her with, "Why don't you tell him what he is doing to you? Then maybe he'd respond."

If Perry set up incentives for Bruce as in (a) it might help Bruce shape up. But there's no guarantee that the relationship between Bruce and his mother would improve. Bruce would have improved as far as his neatness is concerned, but whether this would change his values is doubtful. If the rewards were removed, or if he grew beyond them, it is quite possible his behavior might revert to early Huck Finn. Consequently, while (a) might satisfy the health department for a time, it isn't the best approach to the situation.

Answer (b) is a great reliever of tension for parents, momentarily. It is the way we fondly remember the good old days when kids did what they were told or went to the woodshed for a whipping. In reality that kind of arbitrary rule in the home produced a lot of people who were not able to resolve their conflicts any better than the undisciplined "permissive generation" we have been reacting to for a decade.

What Bruce is going to run into in the real world is a complex interplay of tensions that will demand personal strength in deciding his own values. Imposing Wilma's or Perry's decisions about values does not necessarily internalize them in Bruce.

The old proverb "You can lead a horse to water but you can't make him drink" is in effect here. Parents live out their values before their children whether these values are consistent or not, wholesome or not. Children compare these values to others they see or hear about and make up their own systems. So imposed values are just that, imposed. And easily shucked.

Instead children need to see strong values in their parents, values happily consistent with all that encourages wholesome living. And it doesn't hurt for parents to change, to improve their values as they live visibly and honestly before their children. That will encourage their children to accept new and better values for themselves.

Answer (c) is the other side of the pendulum's swing, in which parents have been persuaded that, being over 30, they really have nothing to offer their children but outdated morals and values the parents are saddled with. With this attitude. Bruce is expected to find his own way, willy-nilly, wandering through the human wilderness without any help or encouragement. Bruce does need freedom to grow, but with lots of participation in the process by his parents. While parents can't push values, they can recommend, suggest, advise, encourage—and live their own values honestly.

Answer (d) has lots going for it. Although it doesn't settle the situation with Bruce, it does handle the hurtful myth that husbands and wives automatically stand united. Such an idea is neither real nor honest—but it is popular.

Answer (e) is what Perry wanted to tell Wilma but didn't. He knew better. Here is a "you-message" which could lead to a shouting session and perhaps worse.

The final statement, (f) while perhaps pushy in approach nevertheless has the seed of reconciliation in it. If Wilma could identify her primary feelings, and decide to deal with them in "I-messages" to Bruce, it is quite likely both Bruce and his mother would both change in ways satisfying to all.

Now let's try to help Wilma identify her feelings. We can make an educated guess as to what her underlying reactions are to Bruce's behavior. If she could think them through she might come up with these:

1. Like a lot of us, Wilma, has learned that neatness is a helpful discipline. She feels Bruce's character would benefit by that kind of self-control.

2. Wilma knows how many allergens and bugs can blossom in the "dust bunnies" a messy room can breed. She fears for Bruce's health, and for the overall health of her family.

3. When she vacuums the rest of the house, she expects to face a certain amount of disarray. But not this disaster!

4. She gets steamed at having to clean up after this hulking litterbug. "He's sixteen, not in diapers!"

5. She feels put-upon by her son, having to be his slave, garbage man, and valet.

6, 7, 8, etc. are vague fears that she is raising a delinquent bum who will disgrace her and bring humiliation upon them all.

But does she explain these to Bruce? No. Instead she demands "for the fiftieth time" that her son clean up his room. She nags him. She reminds him he is personally unkempt. She tells him he's a menace to them all.

She nags Perry, rides his back to whip his son into line: "Can't you do something with that boy?" When he fails, she turns her frustrations full on Perry and the battle is on, folks.

But suppose she were to confront Bruce, on her own, like this:

"It's a real drag to have to clean up your room, Bruce. It's hard work—and I want to get rid of the dust and dead bugs so you—or one of the rest of us—won't come down with something."

With some children an appeal to hygiene or logic simply won't do the trick. They need the stronger confrontation of the personal effect of their actions. Perhaps something like this: "I like my job usually. I like organizing a house to run smoothly, and I feel responsible to keep it going that way, so when I bump into a frustration like I feel with the mess in your room—well I'm frustrated, for sure!"

These are "I messages." Wilma talks about the situation in terms of how it affects her. She expresses *her* needs, without nagging or name-calling.

Bruce may respond by cleaning up his room, because he hears the underlying reasons for his mother's concerns in a way that doesn't coerce his response. But what if he just comes back with more of the "Aw, Mom, you make too much of this clean-gene business"? Does Wilma have any other recourse? Or does she just back up and lay down the law again?

Within Wilma's anger is a demand. Once she sees it and recognizes what it means she can do one of several things:

1. She can *increase* her demand for Bruce to change.

2. Having clearly expressed her feelings (and her demand) she can hold to it or *maintain* it, expecting Bruce to change.

3. She can *negotiate* her need for cleanlines with Bruce's need to find and establish his own values.

4. She can *cancel* her demands and let Bruce work out his room arrangements himself.

Any one of these four possibilities are available to Wilma as a means for her to deal with the conflict. Any one of these four could be the right solution *if it satisfactorily answers (1) Wilma's personal needs, (2) helps Bruce grow, and (3) improves their relationship.*

Let's look at how this might happen for each of Wilma's possible actions.

1. *Increases demand.* This matches Wilma's need for neatness. It may be the very thing needed to help Bruce examine his values and grow. If so, it improves their relationship.

2. *Maintains demand.* Wilma's needs are upheld. May do the same as (1) for Bruce and their relationship.

3. *Negotiates demand.* May help achieve Wilma's needs through Bruce's cooperation, or Wilma may revalue her standards.

4. *Cancels demand.* If Wilma can genuinely cancel her demands and live with a messy son, she should do so only if she is persuaded that Bruce can grow with the responsibility of setting his own standards.

Whichever possibility Wilma adopts she will deliver it to Bruce in an "I message," not the "you message" she has been sending: "You clean up your room or else." The "I messages" might be:

1. *Increases demand.* "I don't know how I can stand to clean your room."

2. *Maintains demand.* "I still feel it is important for me to clean the house the way I think it should be cleaned, but I'm frustrated with your room."

3. *Negotiates demand.* "I want to do something about my feelings about your room, and I'm willing to make a deal that I can live with."

4. *Cancels demand.* "I'm willing to let you look after your own room from now on."

Having made a decision doesn't mean that it cannot be modified and revised as we live with it. The only unchangeables are these basic standards for any choice— (1) that our decision *satisfies our personal needs or demands* (which includes the option of canceling them), (2) that *it helps each person grow,* and (3) that *it improves the relationship.*

Let's summarize the differences between "I messages" and "you messages."

"I messages" reveal feelings without making demands.

"I feel the good work I've been doing isn't noticed."

"You messages" obscure feelings and point fingers of blames.

"You always notice the work Bill does instead of mine."

"I messages" allow the other person to see the effect of

his behavior, without exerting pressure.

"I have an idea that if my work was recognized I'd stand a better chance of promotion."

"You messages" demand action while they threaten the relationship.

"If you keep favoring Bill and ignoring my work you'll regret it. . . ."

"I messages" encourage the other person to grow and trust him to handle the situation with responsible behavior.

"Without an honest evaluation of my work, I don't know how to improve what I'm doing and get a promotion."

"You messages" diminish trust and growth. Although such messages demand change and improvement, the message implies that growth will not happen without the threat or demand being there.

"You're standing in the way of my promotion and advancement on my job because you won't give my work an honest evaluation."

"I messages" clearly separate the responsibilities in the conflict by defining the personal problems and feelings raised by the other's actions, but without making the other responsible for those feelings.

"I feel as if my work isn't appreciated."

"You messages" confuse responsibilities by leaving little or no room for the other to explain his position. "You messages" prejudge the other person and make him responsible for your feelings.

"You don't care whether I do good work or not."

Check which one or more of the following statements seem to be the most useful:

_____ a. "I messages" are selfish statements, "you messages" challenge the person with their responsibility.

_____ b. "I messages" reveal personal feelings and needs, "you messages" tend to place blame and demand action in a specific direction.

_____ c. When conflict occurs "you messages" tend to increase tensions, "I messages" tend to resolve problems.

If you checked (a) you should reread the summary above, because "I messages" as we are using the term would not be considered selfish. Statements (b) and (c) are worth checking, because when you identify and convey your feelings in a conflict with "I messages" the other person at least can see where you hurt and why. And in an atmosphere of honest confrontation of feelings, conflicts can move toward resolution.

Which (one or more) of the following fall short of being clear "I messages":

_____ a. "I feel as if my world is drying up when I hear disapproval in your voice."

_____ b. "I feel as if you are not cooperating with me in disciplining the children."

_____ c. "I don't like it when there's not enough gas left in the car to get to the filling station."

_____ d. "I don't like it when you use the car and don't put gas in it."

Statement (a) is a fairly clear message of how I am reading the messages I'm getting and how I feel about them.

Statement (b) in spite of the beginning "I feel," is really a pretty directive or blaming "you message" which not only accuses you of lack but also insists on you accepting my standards of relationship to the children. If you checked this one as falling short of a clear "I message" you're right.

Statement (c) communicates your feelings clearly without name-calling or putting down the person who used the car last.

Statement (d) may seem to be more of a "you message" than (c) but it is really quite similar. This is an honest statement of feeling and while it may seem a little less tactful, nevertheless if expressed in love, with a concern for improving relationships, is a good example of a confronting style that can resolve a conflict in a helpful way.

How simple it would be, if other people could see things our way! Or at least see that our point of view is a legitimate one, instead of arguing about it!

But many times the point of view we defend so vigorously is faulty and should be challenged. Some of us are stubborn about the ideas we cling to—even the wrong ones—and it takes a brave person *who cares enough* to show us the possibilities of a better idea.

However, it takes more than courage for us to challenge each other to grow through our conflicts. In the next chapter we'll look at active listening.

23
Helping the Other Person

It is a fact of life that some persons are bullheaded, intractable, ornery, in-a-rut, stubborn, malicious, contrary and why did you have to marry one, right? They're just plain mean or _____ (fill in the blank if you wish).

So what does a willing-to-resolve-our-conflict person do with the one who doesn't seem to care any more?

Pray a lot. Try "I messages." Try sympathetic, responsible, caring love. Look into your own life and spirit. Above all turn your life over to Jesus Christ for all the help He wants to bring you in growing in character.

And try active listening. You might find out why the unmovable person is unwilling to move. In the act of opening up the conflict to the fresh air of understanding, you might find your way to the resolution you are seeking.

And you might find how much you share responsibility for the situation.

David Augsburger points out, "In all the counseling experiences I've had with married couples, I have yet to meet the saint who has not contributed to the conflict.

"While the origin of the conflict may be 80 percent

one person's responsibility, the other person quickly contributes his or her 80 percent. And from the point of view of resolving the conflict and going on from there, it boils down to equal responsibility."

"Passive" and "active" listening are terms Thomas Gordon uses in *Parent Effectiveness Training*. In his definition, passive listening isn't bored, inattentive un-listening. Gordon describes passive listening as attentive and encouaraging, with use of words such as:

> Oh?
> I see
> That's interesting
> Uh huh.
> Go on.

Active listening goes further and involves the listener in drawing out the speaker's feelings—and getting to the reasons for the feelings.

Active listening is a skill you can learn to help in a situation of conflict where secondary anger is expressed and primary reasons are suppressed.

We explored the skill as "feedback" in chapter two. The skill involves feeding back to the other person our assessment of the emotional drive behind his expressions, gestures, voice tone, and words.

"Why did you accept an invitation to that party tonight?" Tom's irritation was clear in his voice and expression. His wife Paula tried her new skill in active listening. She responded, "You don't feel like going out again tonight?"

"You've got it," Tom replied. "I'm exhausted. The last thing I want is to get dressed up and go out again."

Paula reached for the phone, "I could call our friends and tell them we want a rain check."

"Wait," Tom stopped her. "Maybe if I took a nap for an hour—we might still make it on time."

Paula defused the situation quickly and positively without an escalation of conflict. She could have tossed Tom's accusation back in his teeth with, "You're always after me to go out," or "If it was an invitation for a game of golf, you'd be there already—but since it's an evening with me, you don't want to go." Instead Paula found Tom's problem was five o'clock slump. Maybe he had a bad day at the shop. In any event, her sympathetic feedback encouraged Tom to accept his own problem with the situation and come up with his own solution.

Allen and Sylvia had two children in school, an old car, and old house, and old bills. Inflation pushed their budget out of shape and, in spite of two incomes, they were sinking deeper in debt.

Allen felt inadequate. He wasn't earning anywhere near enough to provide for his family. And whenever they talked about their money problems, Allen would begin a tirade of angry accusations. Why couldnt' they economize better? Wasn't anyone else willing to cut corners?

Sylvia fought back with her own accusations. Nobody else in the house spent money more freely than he did. She couldn't work any harder than she was doing now. It wasn't her fault the car needed new tires.

One evening instead of responding to Allen's continuing accusations, Sylvia tried an insight she'd had earlier in the day. She fed back to Allen what she thought she was hearing *on his level of feelings*.

Her active listening participated in his struggles: "I get the feeling you're frustrated at the difference between our income and our bills and it worries you, doesn't it?" It was such an obvious thing to say, yet she said it with such a genuine feeling of concern that Allen stopped pacing the room and stared at her.

"Frustrated? I'm just about going crazy, wondering how we're going to get out of this mess." Allen sat down beside Sylvia and took her hand. With her confrontation came a release of tension and they were able to talk over some ideas of how they might deal with their creditors.

Although she used the word "you" twice, Sylvia's feedback statement isn't to be confused with a "you message." "I" and "you messages" as we talked of them in the last chapter have to do with how *we* react to the other person on a feeling level. "I'm worried about our budget problems. I'm frustrated at not being able to make ends meet" are "I messages." "You aren't careful enough with money. You better make our budget work or else"—these are typical accusing, blame-setting "you messages" which project my anger and frustration onto your shoulders.

Sylvia's active listening, "I feel you're frustrated . . . and it worries you, doesn't it?" is a sincere attempt to understand Allen's feelings. Active listening is the skill you can use to help the other person identify his feelings and demands.

"I messages" help you clearly state *your* feelings and needs. With active listening you can help the other person identify and express *his* feelings and needs.

Which one or more of the following responses is an

example of helpful active listening to the following statement:

"One of these days I'm going to tell my foreman where he can go. I can't stand the creep."

_____ a. "You can't stand your foreman?"
_____ b. "If you tell him off, you'll get fired."
_____ c. "I hear you saying that he was after you today, huh?"
_____ d. "So he got under your skin again today, did he?"
_____ e. "You'll feel better about him after a good night's sleep."

Statement (a) is more passive than active, while it keeps the door open for more dialogue, it doesn't help the person identify the inner drives within his anger.

Statement (b) is really a "you message" warning and directing the person to possible consequences.

Statement (c) is helpful active listening in that it feeds back an approximation of the inner feeling in a sympathetic, nonjudging way. If it isn't entirely accurate, the person will make corrections closer to his actual feelings and you will have succeeded in helping him clarify his feelings and isolate the demands he needs to work with to resolve his conflict with his foreman.

Even said in a friendly way, statement (d) has a blaming note to it, suggesting that his problem is his thin skin and quick temper. It will likely draw a defensive response rather than get closer to the problem.

Statement (e) tries to smother the problem by putting it off and discounting its importance to the person.

Okay, you're willing to do something about your conflict, but how about the other person? You want to get him or her interested so that you don't have to do all the work yourself. Maybe it's your partner or best friend or spouse or neighbor or boss—what can you do to start them moving?

Remember, you can't push string. So be prepared to

do most of the initial work yourself. Whatever the problems are, you're part of them anyway. And if you work on your own reactions, you can set up a new situation strongly inclined toward resolution and reconciliation. You can reject your old patterns of frustrated complaining or angry defensiveness. You can take up a responsible stance that removes the obstacles on your part to a healthy resolution of the conflict.

You needn't give up your own point of view to get the other person moving toward a reconciliation in the relationship. *You are aiming for resolution of the conflict, not resolution of your differences necessarily.* There will always be differences between two or more people. That's one of the delights in the limitless beauty of God's creation.

So hang onto your point of view if you believe it to be reasonable and consistent, and not out of step with a godly lifestyle. At least until it becomes obvious to you that your point of view isn't what it ought to be. After all, there's a strong possibility you'll learn and grow from the situation as much as the other person. None of us can afford to be as reluctant to grow as the man who admitted he'd been wrong, but only once—when he thought he had been wrong.

Finally, don't underestimate the power in a positive attitude of strong-minded self-giving love. If you've studied how Jesus Christ lived out His self-giving love, you know He didn't often back away from a confrontation. In fact, self-giving love takes action and confronts the other person with the possibilities of reconciliation.

So in giving of yourself toward reconciliation you won't be giving up yourself. You will be giving yourself toward growth. And calling the other person to grow.

Summing up, to help the other person move toward conflict resolution, we need to confront him or her in a helpful spirit of resolving, reconciling love. Our confrontation will use all of the skills we've looked at so far—

1. *Openness* on our part, willing to express where we are in our feelings and to risk these in confronting the other.

2. *Caring* for the growth of each of you in the conflict, caring enough not to WITHDRAW, or YIELD or WIN or COMPROMISE, but to press on toward RESOLVE.

3. *Speaking the truth* of where you are, clearly—your feelings, your needs and expectations, your resentments and problems, your demands of integrity and personal convictions. The truth you express will cover—

(a) My basic need is _____.

(b) I see it working out this way _____.

(c) I can rearrange it like this _____ (the negotiated resolutions you can happily live with).

4. *Speaking in love,* by using "I messages" instead of "you messages"—"I messages" that state clearly where you are while avoiding "you messages" which blame and accuse, give orders, or specify solutions.

5. *Actively listening* to the other person to help them identify and express their feelings, needs, and demands. *Only when his feelings and yours are clear to you both can you understand your differences. Only when each of you understand what it is that you need and want can you negotiate what you can be happy with.*

Remember the earlier measures which your resolution must accomplish:

1. It must satisfy as much of each of your needs as possible.

2. It must help each of you grow.
3. It must benefit and improve your relationship.

If you're willing to resolve your conflict and the other person doesn't seem to be you should (check the suitable responses)—

_____ a. Swallow your feelings and pride and try and live at peace with the other person.

_____ b. Let him or her know how you feel in clear "I messages."

_____ c. Pray.

_____ d. Try "active listening" to be sure you understand where the other person is.

_____ e. Check your own demands again.

(a) Becoming a doormat or withdrawing isn't going to resolve the conflict, unless it is a necessary action for the time being.

(b) Yes—that's a first step, if you know what your feelings are!

(c) Why not? Prayer has never been known to hurt anyone. If you are not accustomed to praying, the experience could open to you the value of being honest with God.

(d) Active listening will help the other person become more clearly aware of his feelings. It might involve you in more heat momentarily, and it takes courage, but this is almost as necessary as breathing in order to move toward reconciliation.

(e) If you're honest with yourself and honestly seeking reconciliation, you'll see more areas than you have been aware of in which you hold responsibility for your conflict— even if it is only in not being courageous enough to express your feelings to the other.

"No longer, then, do we judge anyone by human standards. Even if at one time we judged Christ according to human standards, we no longer do so. When anyone is joined to Christ he is a new being; the old is gone, the new has come. All this is done by God, who through Christ changed us from enemies into his friends, and gave us the task of making others his friends also. Our message is that God was making friends of all men through Christ. God did not keep an account of their sins against them, and he has given us the message of how he makes them his friends.

"Here we are, then, speaking for Christ, as though God himself were appealing to you through us: on Christ's behalf, we beg you, let God change you from enemies into friends!" (2 Corinthians 5:16-20, TEV).

Part V
Setting New Conflict Patterns

24
Daring to Change

I get tired of hearing people saying that so-and-so "had to" get a divorce because they found out that they had "incompatible personalities." As a trained Christian psychiatrist, I can honestly and emphatically say that this excuse is no more than a cop-out used by couples who are too proud and lazy to work out their own hang-ups. Instead of facing them, they run away by divorcing and remarrying. Then there are four miserable people instead of just two.

Why spread misery? Bad marriages are contagious! . . . I have seen scores of marital conflict cases . . . including many where adultery was an additional factor. In all the cases where both marriage partners agreed to come in for at least four sessions together (even if they had already filed for divorce), not a single couple has ended up getting a divorce.

Not only have these couples chosen not to divorce, but in every case—once they got over the hurdle of deciding to make the best of their present marriage—significant improvements have been made in their marital and other relationships. —*Paul D. Meier, MD,* in *Divorce Is Never Necessary.**

Not every marriage or family counselor will agree with

---

*Quoted by permission from *Action* (Fall 1975), the official publication of the National Association of Evangelicals.

Paul Meier's optimism, One consultant felt that Meier had not been in practice quite long enough to see the inevitable happen.

Yet the point Meier makes is notable: divorce is a lot more unnecessary than people believe. Furthermore, Meier has shown in the scores of conflict cases he has counseled, including situations of adultery, that divorce is not the inevitable answer—even when the couples had already filed for divorce.

So if marriages that are on the rocks can be restored by use of conflict skills which build relationships, imagine what can happen to an "ordinary" marriage by learning the same skills. Or to a business relationship. Or to the everyday conflicts in a neighborhood. With the skills available to us we can learn to manage our responses in a conflict. Also, we can learn to help the other person change his responses.

But we must first answer the question of whether it is legitimate to try to modify the other person in this way. Isn't the attempt to change the way another person acts something like playing God in his life? Yes. And no. To attempt to recreate another person after our own image is a risky business at best, and it is likely this world can stand only one of each of us at a time. But that is not what is involved here.

The fact remains that we do change each other, particularly those who live in close relationships in a family. Husbands change wives. And wives change husbands. Fathers and mothers influence the shape of their sons and daughters—although perhaps not as much as they might, nor in the appropriate directions. Even people who work together exert powerful influences for change in each other's lives.

It would be better to recognize and accept the responsibility to change each other in ways that are healthy and appropriate to a growing mutuality in relationship. And the ability to develop healthy relationships is what Jesus Christ described as a major evidence of a working faith. Because it is only through self-giving love—Christ's kind of love—that we can safely participate in the change of another person.

Let's back up a moment to see this from the perspective of the Bible. One of the central concepts of Christianity is that God changes the persons who commit themselves to Him. We don't know precisely how it happens, but as we observed before, the experience of countless people over the centuries testifies to the reality of the process.

We try to change people to conform to our ideas of how they should be. So does God. But there the similarity ends. Our ideas of what the other person should do or how he should act may be an improvement or an imprisonment. We may be setting the other person free of behavior patterns that are restricting his development, or we may be simply chaining him up in another behavioral bondage. So even with the best of motives our attempts to change others bring us into an area "where angels fear to tread." Yet tread we must! And we tread with safety only as we walk in the love and mercy and justice of God.

The people who saw themselves as the "right" personality changers in the times of Jesus were the Pharisees, a predominant sect of religious leaders among the Jews. With the approval of the teachers of the law, they sought to redirect the lives of fellow Jews. But they lacked a balance of mercy, love, and justice, so the product of their efforts also suffered, as Jesus points out:

"Woe to you, teachers of the law and Pharisees, you hypocrites! You travel over land and sea to win a single convert, and when he becomes one, you make him twice as much a son of hell as you are" (Matthew 23:15, NIV).

The changes God works in us are always freeing, freeing to become that which He has created us to be. As Paul described the process to the Christians at Corinth, "Now the Lord is the Spirit, and where the Spirit of the Lord is, there is freedom. And we ... are being transformed into his likeness" (2 Corinthians 3:17, 18, NIV).

So in our conflicts, the pressures we exert must free the other rather than bind, and encourage the other to grow also in the love and mercy and justice of God. It becomes then not whether you will influence the other to change, but how, and in what direction.

It is not wise to try to change another person. True or false?

False. It is not only wise but necessary in many cases. But there are qualifying factors about our motivations. Some people don't care whether it is wise or not and go right ahead trying to change their spouses or children or associates to satisfy a selfish concern. In that case it will be the sheerest good fortune if the changes they wish to impose are appropriate to the other person. That is why it is so important to have some other values besides that which we dream up ourselves. Jesus Christ pointed to the values of God as specifics for us to use: His kind of self-giving love, and the other characteristics as listed in Paul's letter to the Galatian Christians, "Joy, peace, patience, kindness, goodness, faithfulness, gentleness, self-control" (Galatians 5:22, 23, RSV).

These are qualities of a life changed by God, taught and strengthened by His Spirit. If you are motivated by these spiritual graces—including forgiveness and mercy—then you have a lot more going for you in attempting to change another's habits or behavior.

Finish the sentence with the appropriate comment. One of the central concepts of Christianity is that—

_____ a. People cannot be changed.

_____ b. People can change their lives into the image of God.

_____ c. God changes the persons who commit themselves to Him.

If you have caught the thrust of the New Testament you will know that (a) is incorrect. In fact, unless a person is changing and growing into the image or character of God, he has yet to taste life as it can be for him. Choice (c) is the most suitable of the statements because while we may desire to change into the image of God (b), we have very superficial ideas of what that really means. We can be changed only as we willingly commit ourselves to Him, perhaps in this way as an example: "Lord, You know who You are better than I do, and You know where I am better than I do, so begin to recreate me as only You know how."

When we have in mind to change someone else's life, we should be aware of the need of continuing growth ourselves. Furthermore, it is important to know that in all of our relationships—and conflicts—God may be using the other person to show us who we are and where we are in relation to His character and our potential.

The relationships in which you find yourself at home or at work are the way they are partly because of how you respond to the situations which occur in that relationship. If it is good, you have shared in it. If it is a bad relationship, you are partly at fault. No matter how difficult or despicable the other person has been, how you have reacted has contributed to the present state of the relationship.

And how you react now determines the direction the relationship will go.

If a person chooses to make you an enemy, that is his problem. If you hook in and respond in kind, "You no good so-and-so, I hate you too," you have let him shape you. But if you deal with the conflict and your feelings constructively, you introduce into the situation fresh resources for resolution and healing.

In the following chapters of Part V we will sort out and identify seven characteristics of creative conflict. Next, we will compare our own past methods with twelve destructive fight tactics. Then we will explore eleven steps in how to conduct a constructive fight which can help resolve conflicts satisfactorily.

Finally we will look at three evaluation measures to improve the ability to resolve conflicts.

25
Seven Characteristics of Creative Conflict

Paula and John Franklin went to a marriage counselor, not because they felt it would do any good, but because Paula's lawyer insisted. The lawyer told Paula she would personally benefit from the counsel, and that it was quite possible their marriage could be restored. He offered her the names of several accredited consultants and urged her to ask John to go with her.

Paula wrote a note to her husband, which was as much contact with him as she wished at the moment, and invited him to meet her at the family counselor's office at the time of her appointment.

At their first appointment the counselor listened to a barrage of complaints from both sides. Paula told of John's selfish neglect of her interests. John countered with a report of Paula's overpossessive demands for all his time. John is a producer at a television station and works most evenings. Paula's job at a travel agency has a regular 9:00 to 4:00 schedule.

Paula believed that the television station demanded more time from her husband than was right. After months of frustrated nagging at John to do something, Paula marched into the front office at the station and demanded a more reasonable schedule for her overworked husband.

John was appalled and embarrassed at this unilateral action on his wife's part. He demanded that she apologize to the station manager and back off in her "possessiveness." He pointed out that the evening hours were a necessary part of his job and she had no right to expect him to change his career just to suit her schedule.

At this point John explained to the counselor, "I feel like she wants to emasculate me. I don't know what the guys at the station are saying behind my back, but. . . ." Here the counselor told John to express his fears directly to Paula instead of to him. John turned to Paula and repeated his statement. Paula began to object. The counselor demanded she hear him out, then she would have her turn.

During this first face-to-face exchange, the counselor urged Paula and John to try to identify and explain clearly what it was each expected of the other, the "why" of their anger toward each other.

Toward the end of the first session, the counselor pointed out to Paula and John some of the dynamics of their fight in comparison to a creative conflict which could help them resolve their differences. He briefly described some of the possibilities open to them, and the skills they might learn. In this first session, enough had transpired for Paula and John that when the counselor suggested another, both agreed to return.

Lewis Cozer and George Bach have identified a number of characteristics of a creative conflict that can help you move toward mutual satisfaction of individual needs with a minimum of personal hurt or stress upon the relationship. With some adaptations let's see how these characteristics might apply to the situation in which Paula and John find themselves.

1. *Keep the conflict practical, not personal.* A fight that is only a personality hassle is not likely to have a practical resolution.

When Paula called her lawyer she said she and John were incompatible, even though in their early months of marriage she glowed about how they were "made for each other." Now their fights have degenerated into clashes of personalities instead of practical conflicts that will produce something useful for improving their relationship.

2. *Keep it focused on goals, not principles.* If Paula and John were to pinpoint a goal such as "to harmonize a work and play schedule we can both live with," their conflicts would have been creative. Instead they dealt in philosophical matters such as "the woman's right to work and achieve" and "if a man doesn't develop a career he's a washout."

Like personality hassles, conflicts that quarrel over general attitudes instead of specific achievable goals are not helpful. Insist that your conflicts be focused toward a clear goal.

3. *Keep it channeled, not general.* As the counselor soon discovered, John and Paula couldn't stick to the root problem of schedule, but each of their confrontations branched out into side issues. One which reoccurred was their inability to live within an income any less than they both brought in. In effect, each could threaten the other with financial disaster by saying, "Well, do you want me to get some job on your schedule at $2.50 an hour? You couldn't live on that."

Although some side issues may be vital to a satisfactory meeting of needs, seek to keep your conflicts to the main channel. Limit side issues to those which are pertinent, and keep them in perspective.

4. *Focus on one issue at a time, not all at once.* Often when Paula began to push John about his schedule, he would bring up how difficult she was about their shared housekeeping chores. "You want me to do some of the work, but you don't let me in on the planning," John would counter. This infuriated Paula every time and frustrated any attempt at resolving either issue.

Remember the rule and remember it well—only one fight at a time. Paula should say to John "Let's talk about your beef tomorrow, okay? But right now let's concentrate on mine." Keep your conflicts distinct and sequential, one at a time.

5. *Keep it within a time limit, not open-ended.* No problem is so insurmountable that it cannot be resolved in a reasonable length of time. Some people are impatient and demand instant change. Others like Paula and John drag their problem around month by month, year by year. It becomes a millstone hanging around their necks, dragging them deeper into positions they defend with perennial fervor.

6. *Use varied, not fixed approaches.* Some conflict styles become hardened into automatic responses, "grooves to grapple with," that condemn a fight to repetition. Paula and John could see only one answer, divorce, because they had hardened their arguments and rebuttals into "positions." Each knew what the other would say, thus they concluded that they were "incompatible."

The counselor suggested that Paula and John switch

roles, each taking the other person's side, with him to referee fair treatment (a good argument for seeing a family or marriage counselor).

7. *Keep it open-minded, not prejudiced.* Often we think we know what the other person is thinking—or saying. We prejudge how he will act in a fight, so we are inhibited in our responses. Or worse, we trigger a bigger fight by poking at old wounds. It may be more familiar to keep our fight styles and relationship attitudes closed and repetitive. But conflicts that are open, honest, and freeing are much more successful in achieving needs and bettering relationships.

Richard Walton compares and contrasts open and closed approaches in his analyses of social situations. We can adapt his insight to our consideration of keeping an open, cooperative approach in a conflict:

CLOSED/COMPETITIVE	OPEN/COOPERATIVE
1. Pursues own goals	1. Pursues goals held in common
2. Secrecy	2. Openness
3. Accurate understanding of personal needs, but publicly disguised or misrepresented	3. Accurate understanding of personal needs, clearly and openly reported.
4. Unpredictable, mixed strategies, with the element of surprise	4. Predictable, adaptable, no plans to surprise
5. Threats or bluffs to secure personal needs	5. No threats or bluffs, willing to delay or forgo personal needs

6. Tries to find ways which appear cooperative, yet which satisfy own needs; will use irrational arguments to secure goals

6. Tries to find cooperative solutions to problem; will use logical processes

7. Uses stereotypes, authorities to strengthen arguments

7. Prefers arguments to stand on their own

8. Pursuit of own goals blocks goal achievement of others

8. Whatever is good for the relationship is good for self

Underline the characteristics of a conflict which can work creatively toward achieving the needs of both parties while bettering the relationship:

    a. Deals in personalities
    b. Explores all issues
    c. Works on one issue
    d. Ends in its own time
    e. Varies approach to issue
    f. Seeks practical outcome
    g. Open and freeing
    h. Doesn't drag in other arguments
    i. Is brought to a satisfactory end in suitable time
    j. Sets a goal
    k. Avoids philosophizing

If you underlined all but (a), (b), and (d) you are correct.

Fill in the blank:
An open approach to conflict is _____
and doesn't hold any surprise tactics or secret strategies.

    a. Misrepresented   d. Predictable
    b. Unpredictable   e. Uncooperative
    c. Threatening

(d) predictable

I do love me . . .
My need to be me, to become who
I am, is infinitely precious to me.
I equally love you . . .
Your need to be you, to become all
You can be is equally precious to me.
I show that love . . .
By owning that the thoughts I think,
The words I speak, the actions I take
Are mine—for them I am fully responsible.
I show that love
By seeing the thoughts you think,
The words you speak, the actions you
Take are yours, for them you are
fully responsible.
I am aware that within any resentment
I feel in our relationship is my
Demand that you change—that
You think, act, feel as I prescribe.
I here and now cancel that demand.
You are not in this world to live as I
prescribe, nor I as you prescribe.
But I will do all I can to find you.
Please do all you can to find me—
for this is love.

—*David Augsburger*

26
Some Additional Destructive Tactics

When people quarrel, that which happens depends largely on the tactics each person has developed over the years. Unless we are fortunate in our choice of parents and happen to be born into a family with healthy fight styles, we have likely learned by observation one or several destructive devices.

Counselors meet these same tactics in people again and again. Each counselor has come to know these familiar devices—even to the point of giving them names:

1. *"If Only You . . ."* or *Passing the Buck.* The person fights defensively by accusing the other of causing his problem. "I wouldn't drink so much if only you. . . ."

2. *Undermining, Crisis-making, or the Scare Package.* Playing on the insecurities or emotional wounds of the other. "If I walked out tomorrow, where would you be?" "Your father had the same problem and look what it got him!" "With inflation the way it is, you're going to have to do something about the way you throw money around."

3. *Double-binding or Heads I Win, Tails You Lose.* This is one of the fight tactics George Bach identifies as "Crazymaking," driving the other person to distraction.

"I let you choose the color—and look, it's awful! You did it to spite me!" "Yes, I said you could go bowling, but you knew I wanted us to go to a movie."

4. *Sidestepping or Let's Not Fight, Dear.* Refusing to face the need for change and denying the problem. This is similar to—

5. *The Feeling Neutralizer*—"Cheer up." "Don't cry; think of something else." "Simmer down; let's be objective."

6. *Dirty Pool, Fouling, or Hitting Below the Belt.* Using intimate knowledge of the other's weak spots and going straight for them in a fight in order to disable the opponent.

7. *Withholding or Drying Up the Well.* Becomes a threat the second and following times it is used as the fighter punishes the opponent by holding back on affection, approval, or privileges as a result of a fight.

8. *Playing Analyst, Mind Reading, or I Know You Better Than You Do.* Insists on explaining what the other's feelings are or what the other's words "really mean."

9. *Chain Reacting or the Red Herring.* When attacked, dragging in unrelated issues to confuse the opponent. "Yeah? Well I don't like the way you. . . ."

10. *Gunnysacking, the Super Scoopful, or Circuit Overload.* Attacking an opponent with an enormous load of grievances saved up for D-Day, burying the other's grievance in a pile of counter-grievances.

11. *Carom Fighting.* Attacking indirectly by cutting at some person, idea, value, activity, or object the opponent loves or stands for. "Yeah? Well I don't understand how you can like that stupid game of football—a bunch of meatheads who can't do anything better than. . . ."

12. *Aborting or the Early Apologizer.* Short-circuiting

the fight by offering or asking forgiveness without going through the conflict and working out the differences.

Match the following statements with the destructive tactics they represent from the list below:

_____ a. "You don't understand and that's your big problem—but even if you did you wouldn't do it right anyway."

_____ b. "If we let her go to camp and something happens it'll be your fault."

_____ c. "I'll be delighted to spend time with you and the kids when you get off my back about it."

_____ d. "Hey, baby, cool it. Let's talk about something else."

1. If Only You
2. Undermining or Crisis-making
3. Heads I Win, Tails You Lose

4. Sidestepping
5. Feeling Neutralizer
6. Fouling

___3___ *(a) Putting a person in such a double bind leaves him no way out.*

___2___ *(b) Undermining or predicting dire consequences takes unfair advantage of the other's fears.*

___1___ *(c) "If only you" or passing the buck for personal faults is a tactic used to avoid responsibility. This situation could also include fouling (6), if the feelings of need for companionship are construed as a weakness.*

__4 or 5__ *(d) Sidestepping or neutralizing feelings maintains an unhealthy state of tension upon a relationship.*

Match the following statements with the destructive tactics they represent from the list below:

_____ a. "Look, I'm sorry if I've done something to make you angry. Forgive me—but let's not fight."

_____ b. "You hope you're fooling me, but I know what you're planning. . . ."

_____ c. "And still another thing that bugs me is the way you . . ."

7. Withholding	10 Super Scoopful
8. Mind Reading	11. Carom Fighting
9. Chain Reacting	12. Aborting

<u> 12 </u> *(a) Aborting a fight leaves the other person frustrated and the situation unchanged.*

<u> 8 </u> *(b) Mind reading seriously distorts clear communicating in a conflict.*

<u>9 or 10</u> *(c) Chain reacting or dumping a Super Scoopful on a fight partner creates an impossible situation. One problem at a time is enough to deal with in a practical way.*

A destructive tactic is easy to identify and cure. True or false?

Would that it were so! False.

Destructive fighting habits at best weaken a relationship. At their worst, these devices can destroy whatever strength remains and bring about the total collapse of good will between the persons or parties. These dysfunctional tactics produce anxiety, increase defensiveness, heighten frustration, encourage counterattack, and can lead to rejection or withdrawal.

Produces Anxiety. Whether or not the accusations dumped in a Super Scoopful are true, the long-range effect can induce guilt and anxiety. When other charges besides the one being argued are brought in (Red Herring, Carom Fighting) the other person tends to develop sensitivity in those areas.

Increases Defensiveness. Whenever one person feels he is being manipulated or unjustifiably abused, he tends to build up his defenses. In turn this shrinks the prospects for resolution.

Heightens Frustration. Many tactics ("If only you . . .", Heads I Win, Tails You Lose, Sidestepping, Neutralizing, Dirty Pool, Playing Analyst, Aborting) can build up tremendous frustration. Each of these can be seen as devices to gain the advantage in a WIN style, or to establish a better bargaining position for COMPROMISE.

Encourages Counterattack. If the person is continuously put on the defensive and frustrated, destructive tactics can backfire in a destructive counterattack. Then the hope of resolution is further diminished.

Consequently destructive tactics in conflict are a *double* problem. The person who uses them is crippled in the ability to develop good relationships and the tactics he employs tend to weaken his opponent's abilities to help the relationship also.

How can we cope with the bad habits of fighting? Here is where our motives come under judgment. Being willing to get rid of them isn't quite enough—as the old saying puts it, "The road to failure is paved with good intentions."

The integrating, reconciling strength of self-giving love is needed to bring vitality to our intentions. And if we are on the receiving end of some destructive tactics, self-giving love can strengthen our courage to show the other person what he's doing.

We need to help each other spot these tactics. "I messages" can play them back to the other person and invite an appropriate response.

For instance, we might say to the Super Scooper, Carom Fighter, or Chain Reactor: "I think from what I hear that I have some faults I'd better do something about—but I'd like to point out that for now this just changes the subject. Couldn't we narrow in on. . . ."

Or an "I message" could explicitly challenge the tactic we perceive the other using. For instance, to the strategist who puts you in a double bind you might respond: "I find myself in a real bind by what you say and I don't like the feeling. At first I felt your encouragement to do what I did, but now I feel condemned for doing it. That's a tactic I don't know how to handle."

The other side of the coin is that there are constructive tactics to use. While we will look at an overall plan for a constructive conflict in the next chapter, let's take a look at three constructive personal approaches or attitudes now. You will be developing a helpful fight method when you are willing to take some risks.

1. *Risk spontaneity.* Remember all the times you rehearsed a fight? You planned how to say what you'd say? Forget it. While there is real value in thinking through your problem or viewpoint, don't try to win the argument before it starts. The other person may sense that you've prepared a speech and go on the defensive.

Instead, risk yourself in remaining spontaneous. No predetermined strategies, just bring an honest willingness to solve the present situation.

2. *Risk empathy.* Frozen problems tend to melt in an atmosphere of warm empathetic support. For some people a quarrel degenerates into cold neutralizing distance, reducing the hope of resolution. But if you hang in there, and the other person senses your supportive empathy, then resolution can move closer.

3. *Risk equality.* Strategies that manipulate or dominate imply "I know more," or "I'm better able," or

"I can overpower your position." Everybody loses in an unequal fight, so avoid a position of authority or superiority. Risk honest equality. Let your willingness to achieve resolution and reconciliation on an equal footing be clearly visible.

> Your own destructive tactics can best be identified by (finish the sentence with the suitable statement)—
>
> _____ a. Reading about it
> _____ b. Asking your fight partner

> *Statement (b) is correct. Although you may see your own habits in several of the examples given in this chapter, some of your methods may yet be hidden to you. But you can be sure your partner knows them! Also notice the terms "fight partner" and "opponent." In destructive conflicts the term opponent describes the attitude of one or both fighters toward the other. But in constructive conflict, where a fight is seen as a good means to a positive end, the experience is shared in a partnership of skills.*

> Which of the following tend to increase (I) or decrease (D) the possibility of conflict resolution?
>
> _____ a. Warmth and support
> _____ b. Equality
> _____ c. Rehearsing strategy
> _____ d. Feelings of superiority
> _____ e. Spontaneity

> *a. I, b. I, c. D, d. D, e. I*

It is possible to change the pattern of your conflicts by changing and improving your attitude and responses. Then you are in an excellent position to influence the other person to improve his or her conflict skills as well.

Now let's get into the blueprint for a constructive conflict.

27

Plan for a Constructive Conflict

Argument, confrontation, intense discussion of differences, fair fight, creative conflict—call it what you like, this is *it*. Freed from destructive fight tactics and high-wall defenses, the resolution of differences can be a rewarding experience for both of you.

Make no mistake, your emotions will be aroused, *as they ought to be*. But if you follow diligently and faithfully the plan here outlined, you will begin to resolve conflicts which in the past have only created distance and harsh feelings between you.

The plan is structured for husbands and wives, principally because the most common conflicts in our society are found in the intimate tensions of marriage. We hope those whose conflicts are strongest in other situations will adapt the plan accordingly.

For couples, we urge you to study the plan together, since it can only be practiced as a mutually accepted method. Practice on a minor issue, taking the role of fight-initiator in turn.

This outline is adapted from the pioneering work in conflict resolution of George R. Bach, with additional insights from David Augsburger's work with families and his students at Northern Baptist Seminary in Chicago. Also included are some insights from the methods outlined by William J. Lederer and Don D. Jackson in their book, *The Mirages of Marriage*.

A. Preliminary

1. *Schedule the conflict at the best time and place.* If it seems calculating to you to schedule a fight, remember that most skirmishes go off like a Roman candle, and produce highly negative results—which is one of the reasons most couples are afraid to fight. While it is good to be capable of handling your emotions spontaneously during a conflict, a scheduled confrontation on what might be an emotional issue can remove some of the heat ahead of time.

So think of this as "a constructive debate to solve one of our problems." You can put it like this, "I want to engage you in a fair fight to try to bring about a change."

Pick a time which suits you both, not just before dinner or as someone is going out the door to go to work. Understandably, the one who is calling for the confrontation must be willing to give up a favorite television program or a tennis match.

Select neutral territory, the family room perhaps, or a walk outdoors. Bedrooms and kitchens have psychological disadvantages for some couples. Some counselors believe a couple should get a babysitter if they have children, then rent a motel room. The very factor of cost emphasizes the importance of the date they have made together, and the absence of interruptions and familiar surroundings enhances their need to work together.

2. *Define your conflict clearly.* Do this in two stages; first, as you request a debate-fight with your

partner, explain briefly what your beef is so the other isn't left wondering what it's all about.

Then take time to think through your beef with care. Sharpen it to its basic terms without side issues. You will then be able to state it most clearly as you begin at the appointed time.

B. *During the Conflict*

1. *State your beef and how it has hurt you.* This is like taking a swim, you don't like to get into cold water inch by inch, but you don't like to jump in all at once either. Here is where having thought it through clearly will help.

Make your statement with warm concern for a growing relationship. State it clearly and simply. Avoid judgment or blaming statements. An outline that has been helpful to many is—

(a) "The behavior I observe you doing that I would like you to change is _____."

(b) "It's impact on me is _____."

(c) "When you do it I feel _____."

2. *Ask for feedback of your beef from the other* to make sure you have been understood. Avoid expanding the fair-fight at this point, although it will be a temptation to begin explaining and arguing and refuting right away. Instead make this a ground rule before you start.

Remember, although this plan is structured for a "beefer" and a "beefee," it is a plan you should mutually accept for the purpose of resolving all your conflicts on both sides. We are assuming that, like most conflicts, there are two sides and resolution will not be tilted in favor of either. It is not "I win—you lose," but "we both win."

3. *Now develop your demands and expectations.* Remember "I messages" and "you messages"? Here is where you will need to be very precise in stating your needs with "I messages." Your wife reads in bed, but the light keeps you awake. "When you read in bed, I can't go to sleep" puts the blame on her. A good "I message" would be "I can't go to sleep with the light on. I want to go to sleep and if I can't I get frustrated; then I start getting angry—then for sure I can't get to sleep. But I need my rest and I'd like it if we could both go to sleep at the same time. But I'll settle for some other arrangement if we can work it out."

4. *Rebuttal and interplay of arguments.* Here is where the fair-fight is engaged as each gives full expression to their feelings, openly and honestly, again in "I messages" without blaming the other.

There are two other factors to be sure of here—

(a) Feed back each other's arguments to be certain neither of you is reading into the other's statements something that isn't there. Aroused emotions can distort what you think you hear, so check it out!

(b) Slow down your responses. Don't rush in with a judgment. Trust the other person to be making sense from his point of view. Try and understand. Take time to empathize—feel with the other person. Listen carefully and with respect.

5. *Respect each other's "easily-hurt" areas.* Refuse to hit below the belt. Keep the fight in fair territory.

Trust and risk go hand in hand at this point. Each of you is risking rejection and greater distance between you. Each of you must trust the other to protect each other's trust.

6. *Check out where each of you are.* One or both of

you may give up your positions once you see how the other feels. Or one may back even more firmly into a convinced position. Be sensitive to each other's feelings.

7. *Offer tentative suggestions for a solution.* Work these around mutual needs. The person to whom the demand for change is made should insist that the change involves a joint effort and is not up to him or her alone.

8. *Agree on a solution.* Even if you agree only to do some more thinking and research for another fair-fight session on the same subject, that is progress. Schedule whatever follow-up is necessary. Now declare a truce so you can exercise the fine art of making up.

9. *Be open to another fight.* If you have both respected the rules for fair-fighting and have avoided destructive fight tactics, you will begin to expect your "fights toward intimacy" to be less harsh, less exhausting, less injurious, and more creative, more unifying and invigorating to your relationship.

Alvin and Linda agreed to try the plan for constructive conflicts and decided to test it in a practice session. Their marriage is probably average, without a lot of tension, but both were restless with the drab sameness that had settled down on their relationship.

To keep it fairer than fair, they flipped a coin to see who would go first as "beefer." Linda won the toss and she decided on one of the recurring questions she had about Alvin's feelings toward her. She wasn't at all sure about the reasons for that feeling, but she took her courage in her hands and confronted her husband.

"Al, something's been bothering me and I'd like to see a change in our relationship—can we have a date on Friday to talk about it?"

How would you rate their performance thus far? What has Linda done suitably (S) and what has she missed (M)?

_____ 1. Asked for date
_____ 2. For a fair fight
_____ 3. To work for change
_____ 4. In a specified problem
_____ 5. That is bugging her

For a first time out, Linda is doing fairly well. She asks for a date—(S) on 1—but if Al hasn't been in on it, he would be expecting a chat, not the intense experience it turned out to be. Like the great majority of wives, and their husbands, Linda avoids the idea of a confrontation—even when planning for one. So give her a miss (M) on 2. On 3 she rates (S), but in 4 she is vague on specifying the problem so by Friday night Al was uptight wondering what the "something" was. So although she lets him know it is bugging her, (S) on 5, she misses (M) on 4.

With a babysitter looking after their two children, Alvin and Linda picked up some hamburgers and found an empty picnic table in the park. By this time Linda had narrowed down her beef to a fine point so Alvin's uptight anticipation soon ended.

"Al, honey, you treat me like I'm a friend instead of your wife and lover. I feel your work is more exciting to you than I am and that makes me jealous. I don't think you're interested in another woman but at times I wonder, especially when you seem preoccupied and withdrawn. We don't make love like we used to either and that bothers me more than I care to admit. Do you understand what I'm saying?"

Having invited a feedback of her beef she showed much warmth in her smile and reached out to hold Alvin's hand, encouraging him to speak freely. But Al was primed to respond anyway. "I hear you blaming my job for coming between us somehow, and that maybe I'm sleeping around—and that's simply not true! I thought maybe you'd feel something about my job but nothing like this. . . ."

Whoa! Let's check out both their performances, again suitably (S) and missed (M):

_____ 1. Did they choose a neutral place?

_____ 2. With enough time?

_____ 3. Did Linda state her beef with a clear report of the impact of Alvin's behavior on her life and the feelings it generated in her?

_____ 4. Does she state it clearly without judgments or blaming statements?

_____ 5. In a warm empathetic manner?

_____ 6. Inviting feedback?

_____ 7. Does Alvin feed back her message accurately?

_____ 8. And avoid expanding the fight at this point?

Give them both (S) on 1 and 2 for a neutral setting with enough time to give to their fair fight without distractions. Linda had worked through the complex problem she wanted to tackle, but she would have been wiser for their first session to choose a less ambitious conflict. As it is she misses (M) on 3, with a "you message" that guesses at what is going on instead of putting it in terms of the impact of his behavior on her life. She might better have said, "I feel lonely and cut off from the excitement of your life and when I see you thinking and preoccupied I feel rejected."

So instead of sticking with "I messages" like these, Linda slips into judgments and blaming statements, (M) on 4, reading into Alvin's activities some of her fears and insecurities. And although she smiles and invites feedback warmly (credit her (S) on 5 and 6), Alvin is stung by the blaming. He reads her message accurately, (S) on 7, but forgets their ground rule not to expand the fight until the beef is accurately stated, (M) on 8.

Linda had to back track energetically at this point to try and restate her beef without the judgments she implied. After a half-hour of chewing over her complaint she was able to move on to demand. "I want more romantic attention. I need to know I'm loved, and I'll settle for a special night each week." Once she was able to articulate this clearly, their fair-fight moved along quickly. Alvin's arguments tended to support her need with similar feelings of his own so they soon reached a practical solution to spend Tuesday evenings in a special way to break up what had become routine. They agreed he'd plan the first evening and then they'd alternate.

Finally, they both agreed that their third Tuesday would be given to another fair fight, with Alvin presenting the problem.

Now evaluate the remainder of their fight, once more giving them (S) for suitable and (M) for missed:

_____ 1. Does Linda's demand for change express what she desires in terms of a behavior change to meet an achievable need?

_____ 2. And is she willing to negotiate?

_____ 3. How about their interplay of argument? Are they reaching for a practical goal in a way that will meet her need while bettering their relationship?

_____ 4. Do they resolve the conflict?

_____ 5. Has the experience prepared them for another fair fight?

After their rough start Al and Linda come through with real strength, all (S) for suitable. And as many have discovered, the experience is stimulating, renewing, and definitely helpful. So much so they are eager to try again.

Note the significance of the mutual good will and effort they both invested in the process. Even when a couple are not on as good terms as Linda and Alvin, a mutuality of fair play can provide the atmosphere adequate for a constructive conflict.

"Whoever claims to live in [God] . . . must walk as Jesus did.

"Dear friends, I am not writing you a new command but an old one, which you have had since the beginning. . . . Anyone who claims to be in the light but hates his brother is still in the darkness. Whoever loves his brother lives in the light, and there is nothing in him to make him stumble. . . .

"This is the message you heard from the beginning: We should love one another. . . .

"This is how we know what love is: Jesus Christ laid down his life for us. And we ought to lay down our lives for our brothers. . . .

"Dear friends, let us love one another, for love comes from God. . . . Whoever does not love does not know God, because God is love" (1 John 2:6, 7, 9, 10; 3:11, 16; 4:7, 8, NIV).

28

Improve on Your Conflicts

> A couple can learn to learn from their fights; they can
> learn how to keep them from becoming physical or emo-
> tionally destructive, how to interrupt them sooner and how
> to grow closer because of them.—Howard J. Clinebell, Jr.,
> and Charlotte H. Clinebell in *The Intimate Marriage*.

As you experience creative conflict, it is possible to
increase your ability to achieve mutual satisfaction of
need while strengthening your relationship. Here are
three overall evaluation measures to improve on your
conflicts.

1. *How neutral are your fair-fights?* Negative points
are earned by blaming "you messages," derogatory
words and personality smears, hidden motives, defensiveness, hostility, ambiguity. Plus marks come from
clear expressions of feeling in "I messages," empathy,
courtesy, and fair play.

2. *How sharply defined are your fair-fights?* It is almost axiomatic that tension rises with the obscurity of the
issue. The broader and more generalized the debate the
less chance of success. Don't philosophize. Boil it down.
Don't universalize. Instead, pare down the problem to its

barest essential. Split it down and reduce it to a core—even throw away important elements in order to deal with the most crucial issue.

In fact, *if you spend time defining and narrowing the conflict a solution will most likely emerge.* If instead you seek a solution before you have found your essential differences in the problem, the conflict will likely escalate.

Remember—spend time on clear definition of the problem. Understand it thoroughly in its essential nature. You will be suprised at what this will do to resolve your conflicts efficiently and positively.

3. *How mutual is the process?* It is not likely that each person will invest the same interest and hope in the process of conflict resolution. However, it is important to encourage the growth of involvement and mutual concern. Therefore, the most interested must be the most patient.

The goal is mutual resolution, joint involvement in solving the problems (which are also seen as mutual problems).

It isn't a process to be managed by one person. This will be seen by the other as manipulation. Increase the mutuality. Then resentment and mistrust will decrease.

Let's step back and get a broader view of the benefits to you of a growing ability in conflict resolution.

1. For the occasional conflicts that will occur in the neighborhood and community, you have learned some of the inner dynamics of conflict that will help you.

2. For the persistent conflicts you may face on the job, you have some tools to use to reduce the wear and tear on your own personality, even if you can't achieve the mutuality possible in an intimate relationship.

3. For the intimate relationships of marriage or family or close friendships there is the strong possibility that—after you have achieved some mutual skill in resolving your more serious problems—you will be able to move quickly from identification of the problem to resolution with a minimum of tension.

True or false? Intimate conflicts and the growing tensions they produce can be expected to continue throughout your life.

You are right if you chose false, on two counts. One, you may learn to resolve your problems more efficiently before they even became conflicts. Two, even if using the resolve style you and your partner tend to differ frequently, you may continue to have frequent conflicts—but with considerably lessened emotional anguish on the way to achieving your goals.

Three evaluation measures can give you a means to improve your ability to resolve conflicts. They are (check three):

    ____ a. Consider how strong your arguments are to achieve your objective.

    ____ b. Consider how clearly you define the problems.

    ____ c. Consider how many different aspects of the problems you can bring in.

    ____ d. Consider how frequently you fight.

    ____ e. Consider how free are your debates of harsh hurting words and accusations.

    ____ f. Consider how much each is involved in working toward a solution.

Statements (b), (e), and (f) are descriptive of the three evaluations which can measure your effectiveness. Item (a) is really a negative aspect, because to be reaching for the strongest arguments is to be concerned for winning—and winning isn't the point. Choice (c) is the negative side of (b). Broadening the conflict by adding different aspects is to muddy it and make resolution more difficult. Consideration (d) only measures how often you fight, not how effective you are.

What's the next step? To consolidate your skills by going through the experience of a fair-fight again. And again. With each success will come increasing confidence in and appreciation for that greatest of gifts—self-giving love.

"Paul, messenger of Jesus Christ by God's choice, to all faithful Christians at Ephesus (and other places where this letter is read): . . . As God's prisoner, then, I beg you to live lives worthy of your high calling. Accept life with humility and patience, making allowances for one another because you love one another. Make it your aim to be at one in the Spirit, and you will inevitably be at peace with one another" (Ephesians 1:1; 4:1-4, Phillips).

Part VI
Putting It Together

29
Where You Have Been

The skills you have explored in the preceding sections are the basic elements of conflict resolution. However, like a recipe for a cake, you have to do more than read it to get the taste and the flavor.

Practice is the key to cake baking and conflict resolving. You will be best served by working through this part for the selective overview it can give you, then going back through the book again with your spouse or close friend so that you can practice these skills with each other. We can always learn a great deal more the second time around, and with someone else.

These are individual skills, but they only function in a confrontation with another. So in this part we will review some of the concepts in that light.

Also, in reviewing communications between you and your partner in conflict, we will look at a diagram of six equal rights, which you will want to consider adding to your personal approach.

Finally we will explore the place of faith in relation to conflict, as a personal conclusion.

It is quite possible this study will simply make matters

worse for some persons, particularly married couples involved in a serious and continuing conflict. While the book is designed to help in situations that are not critical, we hope it will encourage those in a crisis of conflict to seek professional help.

For couples whose marriage is on the rocks, you ought to have discovered enough to know that your marriage is still worth fighting for! Get help. There are experienced counselors nearby who can help you through to a new and enriched relationship. Ask your family doctor to recommend an accredited consultant.

And whether or not you are married, your conflicts with your world will benefit from the skills of conflict resolution. Again, the skills are better practiced with others. Many local churches have small groups or classes where these kinds of disciplines can be explored together.

Now in beginning an overview of where we've been, let's take an expanded look at the five common styles of dealing with conflicts which we've studied in Part I. You will recall that most of us favor one style but on occasions will find ourselves using one or another of all the styles.

Considering WITHDRAW and YIELD to be lowest in value in terms of achieving your own personal goals let's put them on the left. WIN and RESOLVE are high in gaining personal needs, so we will put them on the right.

LOW IN ACHIEVED NEEDS	YIELD WITHDRAW	RESOLVE WIN	HIGH IN ACHIEVED NEEDS

Now if we divide these still further in terms of concern

for relationship, the diagram will look like this, with COMPROMISE in the middle—

HIGH CONCERN FOR RELATIONSHIP

LOW IN ACHIEVED NEEDS	YIELD RESOLVE COMPROMISE WITHDRAW WIN	**HIGH IN ACHIEVED NEEDS**

LOW CONCERN FOR RELATIONSHIP

With the diagram to help, we can see that WITHDRAW loses out both on strengthening the relationship and on achieving needs. Opposite this, on the highest level of concern for relationship and need achievement is RESOLVE.

Now test your grasp of the styles by filling in the name of each of the styles in the blanks opposite the brief description.

_____ a. "I demand my goals whether our relationship survives or not."

_____ b. "Let's get along as best we can by giving up some of our goals."

_____ c. "I'll give up any benefits from our relationship by avoiding you in order to avoid conflict."

_____ d. "I want us both to achieve as much of our needs as we can, so let's work at it together."

_____ e. "I'll give in to keep our relationship."

a. WIN   c. WITHDRAW   d. RESOLVE
b. COMPROMISE   e. YIELD

True or false? Most people use one style predominantly, but on occasion will use one or other of all the styles.

Each of us becomes accustomed to using one style, but at times most of us use one or another of all styles, so if you answered True you are correct.

At certain times you may find it best to compromise or yield or withdraw, or even to insist on winning an argument—but these times should be risked as exceptions rather than the rule.

Your consistent aim will be to adopt the *resolve* style. As you continue to improve in your skills of communicating your feelings, and in feedback of the other person's statements, you will experience a clearer focus of differences. And as this occurs you will achieve a more consistent and satisfactory resolution of your conflicts and mutual satisfaction of needs.

You will see differences as natural, normal, and neutral—neither good nor bad. As they arise, you will use them as opportunities to develop viewpoints and strengthen relationships. You will not seek to find a middle ground so much as to understand each other and respect each other's freedom to hold differing points of view.

The idea is to resolve the conflict, although you may or may not resolve the differences. In fact you are likely to discover that in many areas you do hold diverging points of view. As each of you experience growing integrity of personality, resolving your conflicts may well mean agreeing to affirm your relationship in spite of your differences.

Diverging points of view can benefit a relationship if the resulting behaviors do not injure or interfere with the lifestyle of the other person. Differing with dignity and love can be a long-term solution when both parties cancel their demands for change, affirm the other's freedom to differ, and appreciate the complementary richness of their variation in views.

30
Six Equal Rights

"I know you believe you understand what you think I said, but I'm not sure you are aware that what you heard is not what I meant."

We communicate to each other out of what we are. Suppose you intend to communicate a message. You are distracted by outside noise and inner turmoil as you select words hurriedly from a store of descriptive phrases that have previous meaning to you, and you try to project your thoughts through your own method of expression—the individual way you put words together, your gestures and facial expressions and emotional drives.

That particular thought/message of yours must now struggle its way through the other person's way of perceiving, through his or her interpretations of gestures and words—and plow through even more distractions—until it is finally congealed as a message. All within seconds.

Little wonder that we mistake each other's meanings!

Each person is unique, a private conglomerate of experiences, *and not capable of being known totally by anyone*, except God. Each individual perceives his or her own experiences in a private and personal way. In many circumstances, these perceptions are "in process," that is, your perception of a past event may differ considerably from your perception of it while it happened. There is a processing time during which perceptions fit themselves into a grid of previous experiences. For some, this process time is shorter than for others. Some come to quick conclusions. Others may suspend judgment altogether.

As you saw in an earlier chapter, in the heat of conflict your perceptions can leap to conclusions based on signals you think you are getting—which may be way off the mark. And your own feelings may push out hasty and inadequate words to further confuse the issue you are trying to resolve.

During conflict you will be busy dealing with your own needs while you try to respond to the expressions of the other person. You will be feeding back information to the other on how you perceive his actions and their effect upon you, usually while attempting to make your own position and feelings clear.

At this point your commitment to each other to care and to love will be tested to its core. If you care enough, you will put to good use the skills of confronting and feedback and conciliation. As we have noted before, there are at least two points of view in every conflict. And successful resolution involves both parties in mutual respect for each other's rights.

All good relationships involve two-way communication—the mutual right to hear and be heard. Note carefully the dual responses suggested in the chart on the next page.

SIX EQUAL RIGHTS

To love one another is to protect each
other's equal right to hear or be heard

1. I will respect your right to ←→ I will claim my right to be
   be equally heard .   equally heard .

2. I will respect your own- ←→ I will own my sole responsi-
   ership to your side of the   bility for my side of the dia-
   dialogue, and refuse to   logue, and refuse to let you
   carry on both sides by   speak for me.
   myself.

3. I will stop myself from ←→ I will not try to match your
   speaking to my image of   image of me, I am free to
   you, and not demand   change what I was and
   that you be what you   choose who I will be.
   were or what I want you
   to be.

4. I will not anticipate your ←→ I will not bait a reaction
   responses.   from you.

5. I will expect no more ←→ I will not withhold or distort
   than a clear statement of   my views and feelings.
   your views and feelings.

6. In no way do I want to ←→ In no way do I want to
   hamper your freedom for   squander my freedom for
   you to be truly you when   me to be truly me when I
   you are with me .   am with you .

All good relationship
is two-way communication.

Marcie and Frank had survived a near miss with the divorce court and were on their second year of reconciliation around a *resolve* style of handling their conflicts. But a new situation cropped up which severely tested their new life together.

Rebecca, their daughter, was in third grade at a nearby school. The school board now proposed—in order to meet federal regulations—to bus the students to a larger integrated school on the other side of town. Frank spoke in favor of the idea when it was detailed at a special meeting of the parents' association. When they got out to the car, Marcie exploded, "Frank, that's the stupidest thing I've heard you say in a year! I could hardly stand it in the meeting but out of respect for what we've been trying to do, I kept quiet!"

> Marcie will probably regret the judgment of Frank she expressed when her mind catches up to her tongue, but she is doing one constructive thing in her outburst. Can you pick it out of the following?
> _____ a. She is expressing her anger.
> _____ b. She is expressing her need.
> _____ c. She is claiming the right to be heard.

Just expressing anger isn't a constructive function in conflict. And she really hasn't gotten around to a clear expression of her need or even her viewpoint so you would not have checked (a) or (b). Now, however much she has steamed up her windows, Marcie is claiming the right to be heard. She could have saved them both this experience if she had spoken her contrary opinions at the meeting. But Marcie has a residual feeling that the two of them should agree on such a vital issue, that they should stand together on it.

"You know it won't work," Marcie went on. "When

Becky gets on that bus, those white kids are going to push her around. And for what? You're thinking like a white man again, black boy—"

Frank interrupted, "Stop it! Stop speaking to that old image you had of me! I've never made that mistake and you know it now—"

> What is Frank doing here?
> _____ a. Confronting Marcie with an "I message" about his feelings.
> _____ b. Demanding the freedom to be himself.
> _____ c. Defining the issue between them.
> _____ d. Refusing to accept her image of his personality.

> *Frank is doing what a lot of us do not do—he is trying to keep things clear in the conflict by refusing to accept her image (d). He is not defined by what she thinks, and until Marcie remembers that, they aren't going to be able to start talking clearly about their feelings or their differences (so (a) and (c) are not suitable answers). He is rightly demanding from her the freedom to be himself within the mutuality of their relationship (so (b) as well as (d) are correct assessments of Frank's actions).*

"I'm sorry, Frank," Marcie responded. "That was a low punch. But I want you to hear how afraid I am for Becky."

Frank started the car. "Yeah, I need to hear you, honey. And I want to explain why I think any kid will do better at the new school."

With some of the initial tension eased, both Marcie and Frank have now stated their needs clearly. Now they are in a position to clarify their differences and go on to some understanding. In effect, their conflict has been resolved, although the discussion of their differences remains. Both are free to change what they were and choose what they will be.

For too long we have operated in an economy of scarcity in human relationships. If one is up somebody has to be down. When one wins, another must lose. We have admired—and bought—the art of one-upmanship, knowing that it means a put-down for the other guy.

But with the freedom to be all that God can shape in us, we can move instead into an economy of abundance, where everyone wins. By the grace of God in each of us, there can be enough approval, enough esteem and ample delight in one another to go around.

31
Skills and Integrity, A Personal Conclusion

You don't have to believe in God to learn the skills of conflict resolution, but it helps. A life of faith is overlooked by many people today because they have heard that it is unnecessary to "the good life." Some others have bought the claims of the atheists and ethical humanists that God is an ancient fiction unworthy of the modern person-in-the-know.

The fact is that the view of reality we get from the Bible, even more now than before, is holding up as the consistent, valid, and complete explanation of humanity. The Bible, particularly as it is made clear by Jesus Christ, shows both the potential and the defection of humanity. And to me it does so in a way which continues to hold water, even in the light of the modern explorations of psychiatry and the social sciences.

Jesus brought to us the way of a new level of living that is as old as the original design of mankind. It is the way of open, trusting relationships made healthy by the presence of God in us.

Now, according to God's gift of free will we don't have to operate that way, and the state of the world is ample evidence that a great many of us do not. So in working at our conflicts we can take the route of learning these few skills. Or we can determine to put it *all* together and find the more complete way by first and personally getting back into relationship with God, our Intimate Father. He has been trying in many ways to communicate His desire to do so through His self-revealing acts and providences, both in our own lives and in the lives of others. God has revealed Himself through people who have been given special insights, and who help to develop an awareness of God in others—the Old Testament records these instances abundantly.

And there is Jesus. Briefly, the significance of Jesus is that at a given period in time (it could have been the twentieth century as well as the first century) God took the additional step of revealing Himself as clearly as we could comprehend Him, through becoming a human.

Whatever else the New Testament says, that's about the sum and substance of it: Jesus is the clear picture of God.

Most of us haven't the slightest idea of what goes on inside an atomic explosion. In fact, even the scientists who theorized the thing into reality are incapable of explaining fully the unexplainable, at least to a lot of us. So it is with theologians and other explainers of God's self-revealing in Jesus. How it was accomplished, the mechanics of how it happened, we can only try to understand. But whether or not we succeed, the reality has happened. At a time relatively late in human history, God became a man and lived among us.

Why? As the Gospel of John tells us, He did so to show us who we really are, and how we can live as "God-ones" (or "Christ-ones," Christians, as some began to be called soon after the resurrection of Jesus).

Now accepting this isn't simply a matter of factual knowledge, an "Oh, yes, I see," sort of thing. It is rather, "Okay, I'm convinced; now what?" The "now what" makes the difference, because it indicates a willingness to move toward whatever it is that God is telling us.

Let's back up a moment and see what it is that we are, before we willingly become God-ones. We are very much a complex of influences: parental guidance, sibling rivalries, peer pressures, environmental experience, educational achievement, marital relationship, and job pressures. These shape a character that is us, and it is likely as far from our potential as God-ones as Hitler was from Jesus—but we don't see it that way.

And that is a large part of the difficulty. We compare ourselves with each other and we are satisfied. "I'm as good as _____ and better than _____." But that isn't the point. "Am I living up to my potential as a God-one?" is the more appropriate comparison. And here is where most of us have to admit our shortfall.

So in the matter of resolving our conflicts we are infinitely better off if we can begin at the point of personal integrity as an honestly committed child of God. "Yes, Lord God, I want to be what You want me to be, in every aspect of my life."

As a beginning, that's a good one. But it's no more than a beginning, and we have a lifetime's worth of God-one living to catch up on.

It means being willing to back off of many habitual actions that are negative, dysfunctional, dwarfing actions. Like unforgiving fight tactics or lack of trust or a tendency to blame others for our anger.

It means being willing to discover from God the shape of His character in our own individual lives. How is that done? In a myriad ways, but all of them translated into character, developed in us by the Spirit of God.

"Spirit? Aha, now you're talking mumbo-jumbo!" No, I'm not. We're dealing with indescribables, remember, but not unknowns. Even us mortals give off subverbal, subliminal "vibes" or communications. We can sense tension in another person, coming out of his or her "inner being" or "spirit" or "psyche" or whatever name we reach for to describe the indescribable.

In a similar way God has communications that rise out of His being. And these communications are very real—as those God-ones both in and out of the Bible can affirm.

Jesus told His people in a way He hoped would make it clear that, just as He was present with them to help them, when He returned to God He would send them another presence—the Spirit. As you read the New Testament, this Presence of Christ is there, in spite of the difficulty of human language to make us see Him clearly.

And this presence is closer to you than you may now realize. Present and eager to help you become that fully-integrated person you can be. Like Jesus.

So this is where you can begin to resolve your conflicts with integrity. From the inside of your personality out.

Selected Bibliography

There are many helpful books to read in the area of understanding ourselves and our conflicts. The following are a few of the many. Ask at your local library for those which you feel you might want to look at as an additional resource.

Augsburger, David W. *The Love-Fight*. Scottdale, Pa.: Herald Press, 1973

Bach, George R. and Goldberg, Herb, *Creative Aggression*. Garden City, NY: Doubleday, 1974.

Bach, George R., and Wyden, Peter, *The Intimate Enemy: How to Fight Fair in Love and Marriage*. New York: William Morrow, 1969.

Baruch, Dorothy W., *How to Live with Your Teen-ager*. New York: McGraw-Hill, 1953.

Berne, Eric, *Games People Play: The Psychology of Human Relationships*. New York: Grove Press, 1964.

Brothers, Joyce. *The Brothers System for Liberated Love and Marriage*. New York: Peter W. Wyden, Inc., 1972.

Clinebell, Jr., Howard J. and Charlotte H., *Intimate Marriage*. New York: Harper & Row, 1970.

Duvall, Evelyn M., *Family Development*. New York: J. B. Lippincott, 1957.

Fromm, Erich. *The Art of Loving*. New York: Harper & Row, 1974.

Ginott, Haim G., *Between Parent and Child*. New York: Macmillan, 1965.

Ginott, Haim G., *Between Parent and Teenager*. New York: Macmillan, 1969.

Gordon, Thomas, *P.E.T. Parent Effectiveness Training: The Tested New Way to Raise Responsible Children*. New York: Peter H. Wyden, Inc., 1970.

Harris, Thomas A., *I'm OK—You're OK: A Practical Guide to Transactional Analysis*, New York: Harper & Row, 1969.

Howe, Reuel L., *Herein Is Love*. Valley Forge, Pa.: Judson Press, 1961.

——————— *The Miracle of Dialogue*. New York: Seabury Press, 1963.

Jeschke, Marlin. *Discipling the Brother: Congregational Discipline According to the Gospel*. Scottdale, Pa.: Herald Press, 1972.

Lederer, William J. and Jackson, Don D. *The Mirages of Marriage*. New York: W. W. Norton, 1968.

Lewis, C. S. *The Four Loves*. New York: Harper & Row, 1960.

Mace, David R., *Success in Marriage*. Nashville: Ab-. ingdon Press, 1958.

May, Rollo, *Love and Will*. New York: W. W. Norton, 1969.

Tournier, Paul, *To Understand Each Other*. Richmond, Va.: John Knox Press, 1967.